Memoirs of a Ping Jockey

Kenneth H. Fidler

Kenneth H. Fidler

To Carl

ISBN-10: 0991282906
ISBN-13: 978-0-9912829-0-6
Copyright 2013 Kenneth H. Fidler

Cover Graphics:
Dawn Rodden of Creative Design
Los Osos, California

Compiler, Creative Consultant and Author's Photographer:
Karen Good of Serendipity Studio
Lancaster, PA

Publishing Support:
Knight and Day Publishing
Los Osos, California

Dedication

Dedicated to all the men and women who have served our country and to their families back home who have meant everything to them.

For Betty, the love of my life, for my children and their loved ones -- for family…

Acknowledgments

My name is Kenneth H. Fidler. When I retired in 1990, I made up my mind to buy a computer. Soon after, I was telling my wife, Betty, a funny story that happened to me as a little boy during the Great Depression. She told me to write the story down and give it to our children for Christmas. I got to thinking about how much I wish my father had done something like that for my brother and me and how often I have wished I had asked my parents about their childhood days. So I thought way back about all of the great things I did when I was little and ended up typing twenty-two pages that Christmas. They loved it.

The following Christmas I remembered the journal I had kept during World War II. I printed and gave it to them and ended up with stories to give them for five Christmas's in a row!

Now I am 88 years old. My wife Betty passed away in 2009, my children are grown and many friends have asked to read my stories; many already have. I decided it was time to put all the stories into a book form. Many people helped to make that possible.

Karen Good, a talented young woman who has become a dear friend, started in September 2012 to help me put the five "chapters" together. We spent hours forming the book chapter by chapter with many ideas and changes back and forth. We had fun in the process! When it came together, Karen continued to help by creating the photo of me on the back of this book.

My daughter, Marybeth, showed me how the book could be published. She spent hours guiding and helping me, and she introduced me to Karen as someone she thought I would work with well. When it was time, she found Christina and Cheri Grimm to skillfully shepherd us through the publishing process to completion.

My wife, Betty, in addition to telling me to write my stories down, asked me to read them to her daily as we ate lunch together during the last few years of her life.

The dozens of people who have asked to read these stories over the years have encouraged me to continue. To all, thank you very much!! I could not have done it without you!

Although I can't go back and ask my parents about their childhood days, I can write about my experiences growing up so that my children can have a picture of what life was like for me, their father. Here are some of my memories…

Lancaster, PA
November 2013

Table of Contents

PART I

PART II

PART III

PART IV

PART V

Part I

1

My Birth

I was a complete surprise to my mother and father when I was born in March, 1925 at our home on West Windsor Street in Reading, Pennsylvania. My mother was 42 years old and taking "change of life" medication. Since she was only 5 ft. 2 inches tall and weighed 200 lbs. (she was sort of short and plump) she didn't show as pregnant, nor did she realize she was pregnant.

It was about 8 o'clock on that bitter cold morning and the snow was so deep the doctor parked his car three blocks away and walked to our house. A short time later the doctor came out of my mother's bedroom and told my father, "Congratulations, you have a new baby boy." Everyone was surprised, including my seven year old brother, Raymond, who was next door at Showalter's while the doctor visited.

I have always been laid back. And I have also been lucky – as this story will tell…

2

Growing up in the Depression

There are many things I remember as a youngster. We had no electricity. Instead, we had gaslights on the wall, as well as a little gas space heater my mother (pictured here) turned on in the dining room. We didn't have the luxury of a telephone or radio. We had an outhouse in the back yard, although I don't remember ever using it. An inside bathroom was put in about the time I was born.

I remember a coal hot air furnace and what they called a gas coil in the kitchen that we lit to heat water. We used this hot water for taking baths and washing dishes. It also ran through a radiator in the bathroom to help keep the area warm. Since our family was poor, we couldn't afford toilet paper. In those days, oranges were individually wrapped with a very thin, smooth tissue paper. This is what we used in place of toilet paper.

Before I started grade school, I wasn't allowed to wander far from home. One of my childhood playmates was Nevin R. Miller, Jr. - most of us called him Junior. He lived with his parents and grandparents in a house a half a block away from me on an alley, or you might call it a half street. I wasn't allowed to cross the street to Junior's house, so many a time I stood at the curb and yelled across the alley, "Dunor, come out and play with me." He was usually allowed to come and play and, once in a while, I was allowed to go over to his house if his mother watched me cross the street. A few times over the years, Nevin has reminded me how I used to stand on the corner and call out for him to play with me.

One time, while playing with wooden blocks at my house, we decided to play "Post Office." Someone got the idea to send airmail letters, and we started to throw the blocks back and forth…airmail.

All was fine until one of them hit my temple and cut my head pretty badly. That was the end of airmail.

Another playmate was a little girl named Carol Bocknecht who also lived a half a block away in the opposite direction from Nevin Miller. Her grandparents, Mr. and Mrs. Phares Showalter, lived right next door to us and my mother always called them our facing neighbors. Carol often came to visit her grandparents, so we got to play together quite a bit. The only problem was it seemed like I always got into trouble when playing with Carol. Naturally, I never did anything wrong, but Carol came up with these crazy ideas, and I followed. I guess I was a good follower.

Carol's grandparents owned a grocery store, next to our house, where local folks shopped. One day Carol and I were playing upstairs in the front bedroom and she got the idea to crawl out the front bedroom window. These were row houses with front porches and slanting roofs. I decided to follow her out the window. We started to walk up and down the porch roof looking into every front bedroom window, and then we got the idea to sit on the edge of the roof - but not for long. One of the customers going into the store saw our legs dangling over the edge and that was the end of that. We were both soon in the house for a spanking.

Another thing I remember doing when I was just a few years old was to go off and hide somewhere in the house and let my mother look for me. Once, I decided to hide in the clothes hamper half full of clothes. My mother never found me until I crawled out. She was a little unhappy about my hiding place. I guess she was afraid I would suffocate. We still have that hamper in the garage.

We also had a washing machine powered by water. After it was filled with clothing and water you attached a hose to the spigot that ran the agitator when the spigot was turned on. It had a hand wringer above it that consisted of two rubber rollers with a hand crank. Washing clothes was quite an ordeal.

Although we had an icebox in our kitchen, we didn't use it during the winter. Instead we used a window box outside our kitchen window. It had a door on it facing the kitchen window. That way we could open the kitchen window, open the window box and put our food into it to keep it cold, and we didn't have to buy ice. The only problem was when the weather turned warm, the window box didn't work out too well.

One thing we always had to remember with the ice in the icebox is that ice melts. Underneath the icebox we kept a metal tray

4

to catch the water. It had to be emptied every day or we had a wet floor.

While on the subject of iceboxes, I want to tell you about the iceman, Mr. Howard Wagner. He and his wife were our back neighbors. Mr. Wagner had a big outside refrigerator in his backyard, and in the summer he delivered ice to his route customers. In the winter he was the ash man, collecting ashes from the people who burned coal. People had to dispose of their ashes, so they paid him to get rid of them.

There was only one big problem with Mr. Wagner. He liked his liquor a little too much. He delivered ice to a lot of bars and sometimes when he got home, and he was a little "under the weather," Mrs. Wagner locked him out and he slept on the front porch all night. The Wagner's had two children. Eventually, Mr. Wagner's son took over the ice business.

3

Starting Grade School

I started grade school in 1931 and attended the Schuylkill Avenue and Greenwich Street School for six years. It was about four blocks from home, so I walked back and forth every day. They had a program at school where they gave free milk to some children twice a day. I don't remember if I received the milk because I was from a poor family or because I was under weight. I guess I qualified both ways.

When the weather was nice enough, we went outside for recess twice a day. The teachers lined us up in a row and marched us out to the playground and the same way going back inside. One day we were marching back into school and the hall ceiling fell on us. The worst of it hit the boy in front of me, Robert Roth. At the time, no one seemed hurt too much, but a few weeks later Robert died. They said he had a blood clot in his head.

My father had a job as a plumber's bookkeeper. When the Depression came along, he lost his job and from then on he worked only now and then. He had various jobs with the WPA (Works Project Administration). I remember he worked at the Reading Airport while it was being built. I think he was timekeeper part of the time, and sometimes he was night watchman. I know he had trouble keeping awake. He told me he stood in the doorway to keep warm. A couple times he fell out of the doorway when he fell asleep.

Later he had a job at B.J. Saylor's, a rather large, exclusive grocery outlet, well known for their nice produce. He worked a couple days a week, and rode Ray's bicycle into work until one day someone stole his bike.

Since my father didn't have a steady job during the Depression, everyone in the family contributed in one way or another. When I was pretty little, my mother tried selling "Smart Form" corsets. She had sample materials and sample books, and she went around visiting people at their homes. I don't believe that worked out well though. She also took in washing. She had a few customers who brought their laundry to the house every week. She washed it, ironed it and had it ready for them to pick up.

Another thing my mother did to earn some money was to make doughnuts. She especially did this during the Lenten season, but also did it other times throughout the year. She took orders from her friends and neighbors. It was a lot of work making up the batter for the doughnuts. She sat big rolls of batter on a chair in the front of the heater register, so it would rise. After the dough rose, she rolled it out flat and used a cutter to create each doughnut. Then she had to go back over each one, with a cap from a salt shaker and cut out all the holes. I ate all the holes.

No, I'm only kidding. Actually, she put all the holes together to make more doughnuts. Next, each doughnut had to be dropped into a vat of boiling fat until it was deep-fried. Then it was placed on a table to cool. After that came my job of delivering them. Each order had to be counted out and placed into a bag. I carried the doughnuts in market bags, and sometimes I used my wagon to deliver them.

My mother also made Easter egg candy and sold it. She made great coconut cream eggs dipped in dark chocolate. Just like with the doughnuts, we took orders for the Easter eggs and after she made them I delivered them. I don't remember whether Raymond used to help in these projects or not. I was between 10 and 12 years old and he was between 17 and 19 years old, so he had another job.

4

Mohler's Drug Store

Raymond was busy with his job at Mohler's drug store. Since our father didn't have a job all the time, Raymond was often the breadwinner of the family. He rode his bike to work and put in long hours. If I remember correctly, he started working there while still in high school and often worked until 11 PM or later. I'm not sure what his duties were, but I believe he helped keep the store cleaned up and made deliveries on his bike.

He was also what they called a "soda jerk." This means he worked behind the soda fountain and waited on customers. Raymond worked there six or seven years and one thing I didn't mention was the location of Mohler's drug store. It was on the South East corner of Ninth and Penn Street in Reading, which happened to be on the other side of town from where we lived. He often rode home from work on his bike at about midnight.

Raymond worked at the Bower's Photography store before starting at Mohler's. Bower's did the photography work for a lot of drug stores around town. Ray rode his bike around town picking up and delivering film and pictures. He worked very hard.

Since my father wasn't working all the time, I was able to spend a lot of time with him. I remember I helped him build the back steps in our yard. We also hauled ashes out of the cellar together. Then

we sat down and picked out all the unburned coal to use it again. We called that 'picking coke' and it was a hot and dirty job.

Our house was along the railroad and the Schuylkill River. On the other side of the river was Carpenter Steel. Sometimes my father and I took my wagon and walked across the Schuylkill Avenue bridge and down along the other side of the river until we came to Carpenter Steel. Behind Carpenter Steel was a big slag pile and coke pile where they dumped the ashes and remains from the furnaces. We climbed up the coke pile, picked out all the unburned coke and put it in a bag to burn in our furnace.

These are the things we did when we couldn't afford coal. We were in the middle of the Depression and part of the time we were on Relief, which is about the same as being on Welfare. I remember one cold night, my father and I took my wagon and walked all the way down to the foot of Penn Street because those who were on Relief were each given a burlap bag full of coal. It was a little over two miles round trip, but it seemed like forever pulling that heavy wagon home in the wintry cold.

Remember earlier I mentioned we had an outhouse? Well, when I was about 10 or 12 years old, my brother started raising pigeons. He converted the top part of the outhouse into a pigeon coupe. The top part was closed in and had an opening where the pigeons could come outside into an open cage with screening around it. The pigeons were homing pigeons and after he kept them penned up for a few weeks, he let them out. They flew around and then came back into their pen.

After the pigeons became familiar with their new home we could take them miles away from home and they returned. We also had pigeon races where we took several far away from home to see which one found its way home first. Once in a while, if they weren't good homing pigeons, they never showed up again. I remember the pigeon owners were not too popular if they let their pigeons out on a Monday morning to fly around when everyone had their wash hanging out.

A little later on, my brother decided to get rid of his pigeons. So, Nevin Miller and I decided to raise our own pigeons. There was a row of old garages behind the house where Nevin lived with his grandparents. We obtained permission to use the end garage to keep our pigeons. We had about six or eight for a while including two fantail pigeons for show. We did have a lot of fun with pigeons but soon tired of it. I guess because it was a lot of work keeping the pen clean. It was a nice experience though.

My father belonged to several lodges, which I recall was very popular in those days. He belonged to the "Odd Fellows" and to the Patriotic Order Sons of America (P.O.S of A). He had the job of visiting the sick and he usually took me with him. Since we didn't have a car, we walked, and we walked, and we walked. I got to see a lot of Reading that way.

9

The house I was born in had a ground cellar floor with clay and stonewalls. These walls were white washed to make them look nice and clean. Since we lived near the railroad and the river, there was a big population of rats. We had to be careful when playing outside because every now and then we ran across some. That wasn't so bad, but they chewed their way through the wall and got into the cellar. Although we set traps for them, it was still a big surprise when we ran into one or two.

We also had a big wooden potato box, bigger than a large trunk, in the back of the cellar. It had a lid on it and the potatoes were kept in there. The back cellar wasn't well lit. One of my chores was to go down to the bin to get potatoes for my mother. One day I went down to get potatoes and as I raised the lid I thought I heard something; then, I saw them. Yes, two big fat rats had chewed their way into the bottom of the bin, and they nearly scared me to death! Needless to say, I didn't get any potatoes that day and from then on I was very cautious when I went down to the bin.

Sometime later I did get a dish of potatoes, and I was on my way up the stairs. I never wasted much time getting out of the cellar because of the rats but this time I rushed too much and tripped going up the steps. The dish of potatoes went up ahead of me and as the potatoes started rolling back down the steps, I thought surely they were rats. That was a scary day.

In 1936, I was 11 years old and was sick in bed with a childhood disease. I remember the year because we were in the middle of the 1936 flood, which happened to be extra big and the Schuylkill was overflowing its banks. What I remember most is Ray and the boy next door, Elmer Showalter, playing around with crystal sets. I'm not sure if they bought them or built them, but somehow I ended up with one to use while I was in bed.

If you aren't familiar with a crystal set, it's a radio receiving set operating with a crystal detector but without electron tubes. I was able to connect a wire to the crystal set and run it to the bedspring on the underside of my bed, which became the aerial. Then, with earphones, I was able to listen to two or three different radio stations. Since we didn't have a radio back then, this was pretty exciting.

Near our house was a playground called Baer Park. Before I went to school, and sometimes after I went to school, I spent a lot of time at the playground. I had lots of friends, and we used to play baseball and other games. The park also had a field house where we learned crafts, woodcarving and many other interesting things.

Sometimes, on summer weekends, there were organized baseball games that drew big crowds. This is when my brother and I started our first enterprise. We made homemade root beer, capped it and waited until it had a fizz to it. We took our soda to the ball games all iced up in our wagon. It sold like hot cakes. I don't remember how much we sold the root beer for; it might have been five cents. I do know we soon branched out and started making ice-cold lemonade. The lemonade we sold for three cents a glass or two glasses for a nickel.

On hot days, business was really good. Sometimes my mother helped make the lemonade and it kept us busy. We had to buy the oranges, lemons, sugar and enough ice to keep it cold. We had to cut up the oranges and lemons, add sugar and use a stumper to squash it until we had lemonade. It was lots of fun, and we actually did turn a pretty good profit.

My father had two sisters and three brothers. He was the youngest and his brother Calvin was next to youngest. Both got married, but his other two brothers and two sisters never married. The four of them lived together all of their lives. Born in Robesonia, PA, the family moved to Reading in about 1888. First they lived at 528 Cedar Street, Reading, PA, then around 1895 they moved to 220 Greenwich Street.

The family consisted of my grandfather, John David Fidler, my grandmother Catharine Fidler (Schlegel), Uncle Will, Aunt Ida, Uncle Milt and Aunt Lilly. The house they moved into on Greenwich Street was brand new. My grandfather was a carpenter, and I

11

Our Active Elders

William Arthur Fidler, 20 Greenwich St., yesterday celebrated his 90th birthday by doing what he does almost every day—walking to the Berks County Chapter, American Red Cross, 546 Court St., to perform whatever jobs were assigned to him. From Aug. 26, 1918, to Dec. 31, 1953, he was custodian of the Red Cross building, and since that time has been a "fulltime" volunteer, especially active in packing and sorting campaign supplies. He was born on Feb 25, 1865, in Woiltown, in Lower Heidelberg Twp., a son of the late John David and Catherine (Schlegel) Fidler. Before his employment by the Red Cross, he worked 25 years at the Reading Hardware Co. as a moulder in the foundry, and four years as a house painter. He has smoked cigars for the last 70 years. His recipe for longevity and prolonged activity: Keep your legs moving and keep busy. In 35 years at the Red Cross he lost 10 days due to illness. (Eagle Staff Photo)

remember Aunt Ida telling me how she helped her father lay the hardwood floor even though she was such a little thing. Both of my parents were only 5 ft. 2 inches tall and Aunt Ida was less than 5 feet. Both grandparents were dead by the time I was born, so I never knew them.

Uncle Will was a painter for three years and then he became a molder and worked at that job for 40 years. After retiring, he took a job with the American Red Cross as a janitor and worked for them for 35 years. Uncle Milt was a cigar maker for most of his life. He may have worked at the cigar factory on the corner of Fourth and Walnut Streets. Aunt Ida was a glove maker at Meinich's around McKnight and Oley Streets.

Aunt Lilly was the homemaker and she was the one I knew the best. I used to visit a lot and she was the one who was always there. When I was about 11 or 12, I used to go down to visit Aunt Lilly with my wagon and go along to the farmer's market with her at Schuylkill Avenue and Buttonwood Street. I always took my wagon along so I could carry her groceries home. I used to do this every Saturday morning and she paid me a little something for doing it. Now and then when she knew she was going to buy a lot, I went to her house on Tuesday morning before school and we went to market. Then I went to school from her house.

After going to market so often with Aunt Lilly, I noticed other young boys brought their wagons to the market real early in the morning. They stood outside the entrance waiting for little old ladies and offer to haul their baskets home, for a price of course. I got the idea this might be an opportunity to make some extra money.

Nevin Miller and I started to stand outside market early in the morning looking for customers. At first we had trouble with the other boys who were standing there with their wagons, especially the bigger lads. However, we soon learned the early bird got the worm. So, we started to show up between 5:30 and 6:00 AM before the other boys showed up. After standing at market until about 10:00 AM, I still went to Aunt Lilly's house to go to market with her. This happened between the ages of 12 and 14.

When I turned 14, I got working papers so I could get a job. I had the opportunity to get a part time job on Saturday mornings that paid better than standing at market. After all, I couldn't haul baskets for little old ladies all my life. So, I started to work Saturday mornings at Dietrich's Drug Store. Mr. and Mrs. Dietrich were members of the church we belonged to. The drug store had a large lunch counter where they had quite a lunch business.

My job was to keep the floor cleaned up behind the counter and run errands. Sometimes I ran down to the cellar for things. I hated to do that! There were rats in the cellar and if that wasn't bad enough, I had to go down the steps and walk half way across the dark cellar to get to the pull chain to turn on the light. Sometimes as I walked across the cellar floor, I could feel the rats running by my feet. It didn't take long until I learned to leave the light on the rest of the morning in case I had to go back down.

5

Magazine Delivery Boy

When I was 13 or 14, I became a magazine delivery boy. I took a magazine route from a boy who was quitting. I had a route with customers all over town. I must have been in the seventh or eighth grade at the time, attending Northwest Junior High School at the corner of Front and Spring Streets. After school on Tuesdays I rushed home to deliver the magazines, which were dropped off at my home. It just so happened I got out of school at 2:30 instead of 3:30 on Tuesday. I loaded up my magazines and started walking with two bags of magazines hanging around my neck. They weren't too light. I was only about 110 lbs. soaking wet.

I had my route planned and headed toward the center of town where most of my customers were located. I delivered a lot of magazines right to where customers worked and this took me into stores and shops. Once, I went to the Metropolitan Edison Electric Office building, which happened to be about 22 stories tall. I had to go up and down the elevator to many different floors. It really was pretty interesting because I was able to see a lot of different places. I also went into different stores, office buildings, industries and some private homes. My route ended way on the other side of town on Cotton Street.

By the time I finished my deliveries, I was pretty tired, and I

still had to walk home. If it was extra cold and rainy I sometimes rode home on the trolley car, which cost seven cents. I got most of the magazines delivered on Tuesday but sometimes I had to deliver on Wednesday, too. The names of the weekly magazines delivered were *Liberty, Colliers* and *The Saturday Evening Post*. I delivered monthly magazines called *The Journal* and *The American*.

Thinking back, I realize how much walking I did in the past. As I

14

said before, I used to walk all over town with my father and then with my paper route. I guess I sometimes felt like the postman who went for a walk on Sunday. We belonged to St. Matthew's Lutheran Church and we always went to church and Sunday school. Although my mother stayed home and made dinner, my father, Raymond and I walked to church. Since Aunt Lilly and Aunt Ida's house was on the way, we stopped and picked up Aunt Lilly and she walked with us. Aunt Ida, at one time, had helped to start a mission church over in Glenside. She continued to go there and taught Sunday school as well.

I went to church fairly regularly with my father, but when I was young I got restless. About that time in my life I was interested in drawing. Many a Sunday I sat through church service drawing pictures of anything that came to mind. Sometimes I drew pictures of the people on the inside of the church. A couple times I drew pictures of my father, Aunt Lilly and Uncle Calvin sleeping.

6

The Playground (Baer Park) & the Neighborhood

Between the ages of seven and thirteen, I had a lot of fun playing around the neighborhood with all my friends. As I said before, we played a lot at the playground. We also played around the neighborhood. Back in those days there weren't very many automobiles around so it was pretty safe to play in the street where we skated and rode scooters or wagons. We also made skate boxes which were like scooters but they had a half skate at each end for wheels. One night I went to the carnival with my father and I was lucky enough to win a real scooter. I was so happy! This was the first time I ever won anything and I rode the scooter all the way home. I think I wore a lot of shoe soles out after that.

We used to play a lot of "cops and robbers" and "cowboys" back then. There were a lot of open spaces, trees and woods around our neighborhood. We also had some pretty nice big rocks to climb on and this was great for playing "cowboys and Indians." We used to make guns out of pieces of wood, a clothespin and some half-inch wide rubber bands cut out of an inner tube. They were great and everybody had one. We could shoot these rubber bands a pretty good distance. We got about a dozen kids together and picked sides to have a war. In the winter, we did a lot of sledding. The Schuylkill Avenue Bridge was near our house and on both sides of the bridge was a street that went down along the side of the bridge and turned and went underneath it.

From there it kept going downhill for a good distance and then it turned again and went across the railroad tracks and down another hill into a coal yard. At certain hours in the evening, the city put up barricades at these roads to prevent automobiles from using them so that the children could play safely. They got big crowds of sledders at these "rutchies."

Back in those days there weren't too many private automobiles but there were such things as milk trucks to deliver milk in glass bottles every morning. During the day, hucksters came around with their trucks loaded with all kinds of vegetables. The butcher, also, came around the same way and then, of course, the iceman. You remember the story: The butcher, the baker and the candlestick maker? Well, that's how it was. They all came around to the door to sell their wares. There was even the umbrella man who came around to repair umbrellas or to sharpen knives for the kitchen.

My mother had some cousins who lived in Host, PA. Their name was Guldin. There were two sisters and a brother. The sisters were Elsie and Daisy and the brother's name was Yoder. I believe it was Elsie Guldin who was married to William Driebelbis and they lived on a farm in Host. During these years, very few people had automobiles, especially my family. I do remember, though, a few trips we made in an automobile as a family.

We visited them a few times and one time my mother, father and I took the bus to Womelsdorf and Mr. Driebelbis came and picked us up with his car. I was pretty little then and it was a nice experience visiting their farm. They took us around to see their cows, mules, pigs and lots of cats. I remember going along out to the barn with Daisy and watching her milk the cows. This was the first time I saw a cow being milked. We visited the people at Host at least two other times and one time our neighbor took us to Host in their big touring car. Their name was Billman.

Also, my father had a friend he worked with at one time and he drove us to Host in his car. His name was Willis Reinhert and he and his lady friend took us there one Sunday. I guess my father didn't find it hard to get someone to take us, if they liked to eat and play cards. Elsie and Daisy were great cooks. The meal was always out of this world and they had all kinds of delicious pastries. After dinner, they played cards all afternoon. Altogether, we went to Host three times but I believe my brother only went along once because he was usually at Boy Scout camp.

17

My mother went to school with a girl who eventually married a man named Mr. Wegman. She and her husband had a big family and lived on a farm near Oley. I believe they had four boys and two girls. We used to visit them the same way, either we took a bus to Yellow House and they picked us up, or a friend of my father took us. They raised a lot of chickens and had a truck farm, which meant they grew a lot of produce and sold it at a farmer's market along with the chickens. I think we had more fun visiting the Wegman's because they had children to play with, whereas, there were no children at the farm in Host. One thing they did have in Host, though, was a player piano and I used to play while the grownups were playing cards.

When I was about nine or ten my friends and I used to go to the movies. The name of the movie house was San Toy. It was located at the corner of Front and Green Streets and was about six or seven blocks from where I lived. They were all still silent movies where we watched the movie and read the captions underneath the picture. Also, they usually had someone sitting down front playing the piano. When the movie got exciting, the piano player played something faster or louder.

I went to the movies several times and I specifically remember seeing Rin Tin Tin. Most of the time we went to the movie on Saturday because it was payday. On Saturday every child who entered the movie received a pay envelope containing anywhere from one cent up to twelve cents. I think it cost about twelve cents to get into the movie and it was always fun. The outside of the movie house was really was pretty. It looked to be some kind of oriental palace with fancy peaks and the colors were exceptional as well.

When we were about 11 or 12, a new movie house opened closer to home. It was located in the 600 block of Schuylkill Avenue, only about three blocks from where I lived. The name of the movie house was Rio. Soon after it opened, we found out they were looking for some kids to pass out circulars. So, about three or four of us went to apply and we were all hired. The movie circular advertised what movies were in for the week and we were each given a route where we had to deliver a circular to every house. For doing this, we were each given two free passes to the movies.

7

A Bakery Route

Around this time, my brother came up with an idea to earn some extra money. He was still working at Mohler's but had an idea about something he thought my father could do. He started a bakery route as a Bob Tailer. He took my wagon and built a box bigger than it, and it nested on the underside so the nested part fit down inside it. This held the box in place on top of the wagon without it sliding around. The box had glass windows on the sides and a door at the back end. Inside the box were shelves to hold the baked goods. He painted it and it looked real business like.

The father of one of my brother's schoolmates owned a bakery. He sold the baked goods to my brother wholesale and my brother sold them to customers for profit. It went a little slow in the beginning. You realize he had to buy a variety of baked goods to take around to customers and then sell them and take orders for the next day.

I don't remember if he had to go to the bakery to pick up the goods or if they were delivered to our house. Either way, it meant pulling the wagon with the heavy wooden box on it loaded with baked goods consisting of breads, pies, cakes and all kinds of coffee cakes. As his route expanded, he sold baked goods from more than one bakery. Oh yes, I didn't tell you the most important part…he pulled this with his bicycle all over town.

Unfortunately, Father never took over the job. Maybe he decided it was too much for him to pull everything with his bike. I guess it was almost too much for Ray also because eventually he went modern and bought a 1929 Model A Ford for $23. I believe this happened about 1937 or 1938.

The car was a two-door sedan and it ran pretty nice for the bakery route. It used so much oil he used old drain oil from local garages. After it was taken out of a car he got it for free; back in those days gas cost about 12 cents a gallon. Ray finally sold the Ford for $30; I guess he made out pretty well.

8

My Paper Route

When all this was going on with the bakery route, Ray also found me a large paper route. I was about 15 at the time. The paper route was in Glenside across the Schuylkill Avenue Bridge and up the hill about one block from where I picked up my papers. I counted them to make sure I had enough. At the time, I had about 163 customers and my route number was 233. I then divided them up. I needed about 100 papers for Glenside, 31 papers for Greenmont and 32 for Greenfields. My brother loaned me some money and this is when I got my first bike.

Anyway, after I divided them up, I took 100 papers and delivered them by walking eight blocks, which was the upper part of Glenside. I then ended up where I started, and put the rest of the papers on my bike and started out for Greenmont, which was a new development of homes just being built. Doing all of this took about an hour or maybe just a little more. I then had 32 papers left for Greenfields and that took another hour. Greenfields consisted mostly of big expensive homes outside the city of Reading and covered about ten miles on my bike. I had to go up Bernville Road from Reading all the way to the airport. I had just about every house between Bernville Road and the Schuylkill River. On the other side of Bernville Road was the bigger part of Greenfields, which ran all the way down to the Tulpehocken Creek.

It took just as long to deliver those 32 papers as it did the rest of the route. At Christmas time, though, the newspaper company gave all the carriers calendars we were supposed to give to our customers for the New Year. The customers, in return, gave the paper boy a tip for a Christmas gift according to how well they liked you. Some people didn't give anything but most customers gave around fifteen to twenty five cents. The customers in Greenfields always tipped well and I usually ended up collecting as much from them as the rest of the paper route. The paper route was named the "Reading Eagle" and I had to deliver the paper seven days a week. This meant I had to ride my bike 10 miles a day, every day of the year.

I guess I was like a postman...rain, snow or sleet, the paper still got through. I remember many a night when it snowed, I either walked the ten miles or I rode part way through and pushed my bicycle the rest of the way. After school, I rushed home to get my bicycle and then head over to Glenside to pick up my papers. It was usually about 3:30 to 4:00 PM when I was ready to start delivering my papers, so it was close to 6:00 PM when I was finished. If the weather was bad, I returned much later. I had the paper route about two and a half years and I don't remember missing any time due to sickness. I even had a substitute when I couldn't make it for some reason.

There is one time I had to get a substitute. If you remember, I mentioned about my brother working at Mohler's drug store. At this time, the 1939-1940 World Fair was going on in New York City. Mr. Mohler had been over to see it and was so impressed that when he returned he decided to send each of his employees to see the fair at his expense. He also announced he would pay for each employee to take a guest and Ray decided to take me. This was an unexpected surprise for me; one that I enjoyed very much. Hence, this was one of the few times I needed to get a substitute for my route.

We went to the fair on a Sunday and took the train. It was really exciting especially since it was the first time I was ever out of Pennsylvania. We only went for the day, but we went early and stayed late and there was so much to see. The thing that stuck in my mind the most was the General Motors building. It had an exhibit called the "Futurama." It was like a big "Roadside America" display, only better. It had big cities on a platform with super highways and their big interchanges and towering skyscrapers. I saw so many different things that up until then I had only dreamed about. Another thing I saw for the first time was a television.

We were in the RCA building and the television was a big wooden cabinet that had a hinged lid that acted as a screen when it was lifted up almost 90 degrees. The picture screen was horizontal and when the lid was lifted up almost vertical, the picture reflected on the lid. The one sad thing about this day was that our father was sick in bed with a nervous breakdown. He was one that worried a lot and with being laid off so much I guess it was too much.

Soon after I started my paper route, the newspaper company announced that they were going to have a big contest for their carriers. The five carriers who were able to get the most new customers by the end of the contest would win a free trip to Cuba! There also were some smaller prizes like a one day trip to New York's World Fair. Fortunately, I got lucky because the U.S. Government had just finished building a big low cost housing project just across the street from where my paper route was. These were subsidized homes for low income families. So as they started to move in, I signed them up for the paper. It was almost like shooting fish in a barrel. Well, I guess you won't be surprised when I tell you I was one of the five winners to earn a free trip to Cuba.

This created a lot more work for me delivering all those newspapers. One thing I didn't mention was that besides delivering all those papers, I also had to go around and collect the money because I had to pay the bill for the papers by Saturday at noon. I usually collected some on Friday evening but most of it on Saturday morning. The worst thing was trying to collect money from the customer who wasn't at home because it meant I had to go back at a later time. Some people paid me once a month, which helped a lot to cut down on the time, but then there were some that I had to keep going back until I caught them at home or until they were able to pay me. Sometimes customers made me wait for my money, but if it went over six or seven weeks I had to drop them and I lost a little money sometimes because of that.

By the end of the contest, my route had gone from about 163 customers to about 246. By this time, my father was over his nervous breakdown and he started to help me when he could. He had no bike so he had to walk over to Glenside where we picked up the papers. Eventually, he was able to deliver all of the papers in Greenmont as well as the papers in the new housing project. While he did that, I delivered Glenside and then rode the ten miles on my bike and we finished about the same time. That was a lot of papers for him to carry while walking, but he seemed to like it.

9

The Trip to Cuba

Now for the trip to Cuba! That was really something. We traveled in three automobiles owned by the chaperons. The party consisted of the company general manager who was in charge of all the newspaper carriers, his wife and two daughters as well as two district managers, one nurse and five of us winners.

The trip was for two weeks, all expenses paid. I believe we left Reading early Saturday morning and drove to Washington, DC. Don't forget there weren't any super highways or expressways back in those days, so we traveled down old Route 1 all the way to Florida. It was mostly two lane and, now and then, three lanes. We stopped at Washington to go through Mt. Vernon and then went on until we went as far as Sumter, SC where we stayed in cabins for our first night.

The second day we stopped at St. Augustine, Florida and had a drink from the "Fountain of Youth." We also had a ride on a Glass Bottom Boat in Silver Springs, Florida and spent some time at Daytona Beach. After that, we were off to Miami, Florida where we boarded the ship that took us to Havana, Cuba. We left that evening and arrived there the next morning.

When we arrived in the harbor we saw Morro Castle and after that we left the ship. We were put up in a very nice hotel down in the center of Havana. I believe it might have been the Plaza Hotel where we were all treated like kings. I guess it was because we were Americans and paperboys. We visited Havana over the week of the fourth of July and were invited to march in the parade and had our pictures taken for the local newspaper. After the parade, we were invited to the capital and where we were introduced to the president of Cuba. We all shook hands with President Batista. The capital resembled our capital in Washington, DC very much.

Each day we had a different tour. One day we went out to the Morro Castle that was a fortress at the narrow end of the harbor. I remember we were taken down to the dungeons at ground level facing out towards the sea. Some of them had torture equipment and at least one cell that faced the sea, kept prisoners in it while the tide came in and the water came right into the cell.

Another day we visited sugar plantations. We finished our day by enjoying a six course dinner that was more than I could eat. We also visited the Bacardi rum factory where the adults had a rum tasting party, but we weren't allowed to have any. One thing that was popular with all of us was papaya juice. It was a real tasty juice from the papaya tree and everyone drank his or her share of it.

Next was the tour of the Havana Cigar Factory. I found that very interesting because they explained all about the tobacco and how the cigars were made. There were rows and rows of people in a big room who were all sitting at big tables facing towards the front. They were rolling and wrapping these cigars but they all seemed to be more interested in something happening at the front of the room. Then I realized there was a man standing on a box at the front of the room. He had a book and we were told that he was reading love stories to the employees, who were mostly women, while they were rolling the cigars. I guess today most places have soft music playing instead of something like that.

After about eight days it was time to pack up and go aboard ship again for our trip back to Miami. This was the first time I was ever away from home for this long and I really thought I would get homesick. Although I minded it a little the first one or two days, I soon forgot about it because there was so much to see and do. I don't remember much about the trip home but I believe we kept going without stopping more than we had to all the way home. I think everyone was anxious to get home at this point. One thing I forgot to mention, though, was that because I did get so many customers, I also won a free trip to the world's fair. Since my brother Ray had taken me along on his trip to the fair I decided to let him go in my place.

The corner where I picked up my papers was the same corner where two other paperboys picked up their papers. I grew up with them; one was Tommy Parsons and the other was Reynold Bittle. They both had routes in lower Glenside but both routes were rather small and it didn't take them too long to deliver their papers. They were both good friends and we ran around together. I'll never forget one Sunday I was over at Reynold's house and they announced on the radio that Pearl Harbor was just bombed. Who would have thought at the time that we both would end up in the Navy?

About that time, the morning paper boy in Lower Glenside decided to quit and Ray thought it was a good idea if I took that route also. The morning paper was the "Reading Times" and the paper route was much smaller than my evening route but it was just too much. I tried it for two or three weeks and I had to get up in the morning between 5 and 5:30 AM in order to be able to deliver the papers and still get to school on time. Even if I had been able to deliver both routes, I didn't have enough time to do the collecting on Saturday to pay the bill by noontime.

My time was also taken up with music lessons and practicing. I played the cello and my brother played the violin. Yes, I come from a long line of fiddlers. I don't remember why or how I became interested in learning to play the cello but it could have been through my music classes in school. They used to have some instruments at school they loaned out in hopes of getting students interested in playing. I know my brother had a lot to do with it but I'm not sure if it was the instrument I decided to play or if it was what the music teacher chose to teach me. Either way, it turned out the music teacher was a friend of my brother or he came into Mohler's and Ray knew him that way. The name of my teacher was Mr. White and he lived with his wife in an apartment in the Medical Arts building on North Fifth Street, a half block away from our church.

You probably won't believe this but we ended up with a strange arrangement. I took my music lessons on Sunday morning at 8 AM before Sunday school. This meant I usually had to take my cello, which was an armful to carry, and get on a trolley car to be in town early enough to be at my lesson. Then, after my lesson I had to carry my cello to church and walk home with it afterwards. I did that for a pretty long time and I played in the Jr. High School orchestra for three or four years as well as in the Reading High School orchestra until I went into the Navy.

10

632 Schuylkill Avenue

Somewhere in late 1940 or early 1941 we moved from Windsor Street to 632 Schuylkill Avenue. My father had been buying the house on Windsor Street but with the Depression and my father not working, I guess they ended up losing everything. I imagine that for a long time the person holding the mortgage just let us live there by paying some amount of rent.

Eventually, we had to move to Schuylkill Avenue. It was a first floor apartment with a big living room and we also had use of the basement. We entered the apartment from the front vestibule and at the opposite end of the living room was the bathroom. At the back end of the bathroom there was the bedroom and, from there, we went into the kitchen. It was a big kitchen and at the back of the kitchen there was a pantry where we could store a lot of things. It was a row house with a dry goods store on one side and an elderly couple living on the other side.

It was strange having to go through the bathroom every time you wanted to go from one end of the house to the other, but other than that it was a pretty nice apartment. Around this time I became interested in photography and, for a while, I had a little photo shop set up in the basement. It was just a hobby but I was able to develop my own film and print my own pictures.

11

My Father Died

After we moved into the apartment, my parents slept in the living room on a couch that opened up into a bed and Ray and I slept together in the bedroom. Late one night, at the end of March of 1941, I awoke to find the lights on and my mother and Ray were up. My father was sick and they had to call the doctor. After the doctor arrived and examined my father, we learned my father had had a stroke that left him paralyzed on his left side. This was quite a shock.

As the days went by he seemed to be responding to therapy a little bit. He tried to talk but it was hard to understand what he was trying to say. I think after a while he moved his arm slightly, but he still had no feeling in his leg. On Sunday morning April 14, 1941, my father died. Ray had gone to church that morning and for some reason I decided to stay home. I had been sitting with my father and he was trying to talk to me. After a while I understood what he was trying to say.

He said that he and my mother always hoped to do something special for their 25th wedding anniversary. They would have been married 25 years on August 16 of that year. About a half hour after he told me that, he died. There wasn't a telephone at church, so I ran all the way to St. Matthew's to tell my brother. I think I cried all the way there. I was 16 years old. My father was buried at the Laureldale Cemetery. My mother remarked one time that he died on April 14 and her birthday was April 16. My father was buried April 18, 1941.

12

The Reading Times

Soon after my father died, I quit my paper route and started to work at the Reading Times in the early morning. It was a part time mailroom job because I was still in high school. I came home from school about 3:30 and did my homework, ate supper and tried to get to bed by 8:00 PM. Then I woke up at midnight and went into work in time to start by 1:00 AM. From 1 AM to 2 AM, we had to prepare for when the presses started running. As the presses started to run, one of us stood at the end of the conveyor and took off the papers in stacks of 50 and piled them on a truck. Six other fellows took the papers off the truck, counted out the right amounts for each paper route and tied them up in bundles to be delivered to the street corners where each paperboy picked them up. Everyone who could do it rotated on the conveyor.

When the presses ran extra fast, it was a little hard to take the papers off the conveyor quickly enough. If I got too far behind, it could be a mess with papers all over the floor. I was pretty good at it, though, and that was one of my regular jobs. Usually, if the press started on time, we were finished by 5 AM. Sometimes they started printing the paper late because of trouble with the press or sometimes they held up the press because of a hot news flash. When I got back home, I went back to bed and tried to sleep until 8 AM, then ate a quick breakfast before I went to school. The school was all the way up at 13th and Douglas Streets and I took the trolley. This was when I was in 11th and 12th grades at Reading High School, and I was able to arrange my schedule so that my study classes were at about 9 AM.

After I worked at the newspaper for a while, I was given an additional job. I was to stay an extra hour after work to sweep the outside loading platform. About six months later, I started going up to the fourth floor to be the telephone operator between 6 AM and 7 AM along with sweeping up from 5 AM to 6 AM. That continued until I went into the Navy.

Sometime in 1942, my brother joined the Army Signal Corp Reserve and started school in Pittsburgh. At that time it was just my mother and I living on Schuylkill Avenue. I continued to work at the newspaper and go to school. However, month after month I started to see a lot of my friends going off to the service. Some were drafted and some enlisted.

13

Drafted

On March 2, 1943, I turned 18 years old. Days later, I received my draft notice. I was given the option to defer and finish school or I could go into the service right away and get my diploma at the end of the school year. Since a lot of my friends had already left, I decided to leave right away. It didn't take long after that. On April 6, I went to Allentown for a physical and was sworn into the Navy that same day. Fortunately, even though I was drafted, they gave me the choice of Army, Navy or Marines. After I was sworn in, I asked one of the officers if he was sure that I was getting into the Navy and he said, "Yes, just try to get out!"

Part II

BNP 602 (Reserve)
(Revised August 1942)

9

Name ___FIDLER, Kenneth Herner___
(Name in full, surname to the left)

__821 107,5__ rate __S V-6 USNR-SV__
(Service number) (USNR Class)

Date reported aboard __5 - APR 1943__

___A. F. I. C. ALLENTOWN, PA.___
(Present ship or station)
AS-USN-I
(Ship or station received from)

__5 APR 1943__ Inducted into the
U. S. Navy as A.S., USN-I, this
date, in accordance with Selective
Training & Service Act of 1940, as
amended.

__5 APR 1943__ Voluntarily enlisted
as Apprentice Seaman, Class V-6, U. S.
Naval Reserve, SV, this date to serve
for a period of two (2) years. BNP
Form 603 (Shipping Articles) executed

PLACED ON INACTIVE DUTY THIS DATE.

Called to active duty this

Date transferred date __12 APR 1943__

To __Receiverete Sampson, N.Y.__

E. J. _____ Ensign D-V(S) USNR
Signature and rank of Commanding Officer.

__13 APR 1943__

Date received aboard _____

__U.S.N.T.S. SAMPSON, N,Y.,__
(New ship or station)

AFIC   Allentown, Pa.
(Last ship or station)

W. A. BART. Captain. U.S.N. (DMC)
Signature and rank of Commanding Officer.

ORIGINAL

32

14

On My Way to Boot Camp

I was placed on active duty on April 12, 1943 and reported to Allentown. We went by train to the US Naval Training Station in Sampson, NY and arrived there the next day. I remember the train was a noisy and dirty old coal burner.

15

Boot Camp

I guess there were several hundred of us on the train when we arrived in Sampson. They took us through the supply building and gave us our large canvas sea bags, uniforms, bed clothing, and hammocks. We were then divided into groups and assigned barracks. Each group was called a company and given a company number. Sampson Naval Training Station was a large facility divided into 100 barracks numbered 1-100 for one section and 101-199 for the next section, etc. Each company had the same number as the barracks they lived in. I was in Company 159, Unit C.

We all started out with the rating of Apprentice Seaman. The man in charge of each company was a Chief Petty Officer. He trained us even though he was an enlisted man. We didn't usually have to salute an enlisted man, but in boot camp we had to salute him every time we passed him. That way we got used to saluting an officer. Anytime we failed to salute him, we were given special details or punishment. We didn't have to salute when we weren't wearing hats. However, we always had to wear our hats unless we were indoors.

Sampson Naval Training Station was a boot camp and all of us apprentices were called Boots. We were called this because we had to wear leggings strapped around our lower calves for the entire time we trained. It set us apart from everyone else and we weren't allowed to go outside without our boots on until we graduated.

Boot camp lasted for six or seven weeks of training. The normal amount of time was twelve weeks but right before we arrived they started a crash program of six or seven weeks. The majority of the time we did a lot of marching and I mean, a lot of marching. We marched morning, noon, and sometimes at night. And when we weren't marching we were cleaning. It seemed as if we were always getting ready for the next inspection, which happened every Saturday afternoon. We spent all Saturday morning cleaning the barracks and then everyone got washed and dressed in their dress uniforms in time to line up in a long row inside the barracks. We shined our shoes until we could almost see ourselves in them. Sometimes we stood waiting for an hour or more until the inspecting officer came around. He was usually the Commandant of the Naval Base.

When we first lined up for inspection, they took a long string and stretched it out and had us line up our toes to the string to make a nice straight line. Of course, if the Commandant didn't show up within twenty minutes or so, we had to get the string out again. We competed with all the other barracks in our section and the one with the highest score for the week was named Rooster Company. We only got liberty a couple of times while we were there, but Rooster Company was allowed to stay out a little longer. Liberty meant time off the base, usually for the afternoon or evening. About the only place we could go was a nice little town on a lake in Geneva. There wasn't too much to do for entertainment, but it was wonderful to get away from the base for a while.

We were supposed to keep all our clothing in our sea bags and were taught how to pack everything for traveling. It was quite a process. The hammock was stretched out straight with the mattress and bed clothing inside. With the sides of the hammock closed up tight, we laid the filled sea bag in the center of it and then pulled both ends up around the ends of the sea bag to hold everything together. The whole bundle was quite a hand full and rather heavy. It was so bulky; I could hardly lift it, let alone carry it. However, we had to carry the whole thing around the drill field one time. It just about killed us and I think they did that to give us an idea what punishment might look like if we got into big trouble.

We learned a variety of things in boot camp about personal hygiene and keeping our clothes in good shape. For most of us keeping shaved and clean wasn't a problem, but there was one or two fellows who didn't seem to like to take a shower or wash. We eventually ended up throwing one guy in the shower with his clothes on. I think he got the message after that.

We did our own laundry in a room filled with rows of sinks and scrubbed our clothes on washboards. There weren't any washing machines or dryers so we hung our clothes out on the wash line with clothes stops, which were short pieces of heavy string used to tie clothing to the line. That was the Navy way.

We also learned to neatly fold our uniforms and kept them pressed by stretching them out under our mattresses and sleeping on them. That way we were always ready to go. We were given a pair of dress shoes and one pair of work shoes or marching shoes. The marching shoes were ankle high and we completely wore out the soles by the end of boot camp and had to have them re soled. Another important rule involved maintaining highly polished shoes at all times.

It didn't take long to learn how to give them a spit shine and when we weren't marching, we were busy shining our shoes.

Some of the fellows were assigned KP, which stands for Kitchen Police. I was fortunate and never drew KP the whole time I was in the Navy. I'm sure I would not have enjoyed peeling potatoes, washing dishes or serving the food.

Along with these things, we also received important training in the areas of fire fighting and going through the gas chamber with gas masks on our heads. We trained in a cement block building, or part of a building dowsed in oil then set on fire. We actually had to go into the burning building where we learned how to extinguish fires by using various fire hoses and nozzles. They also took a large group of fellows and gave each one a gas mask and showed us how to put it on properly. Then they marched us into a building filled with tear gas. After we were all lined up we were told to take our masks off and take a big breath of the gas. Finally, we were allowed to put our masks back on and they marched us out. What a relief that was.

After a few weeks of marching and training, we were considered experienced and we each received a dummy rifle to carry. We learned all kinds of drills and I especially remember the close order drill. We carried the rifles on our shoulder and reversed direction without hitting anyone with the rifle. Near the end of our training, we had a big parade and inspection out on the drill field in full dress uniform. All companies on base marched at one time past the viewing stand where the Commandant stood. It was quite impressive.

We also took a written test and were marked in three categories so they could figure out where to place us. The first was general classification and I earned a 77.

The second one was arithmetic and I scored a 95. The third category was English. I received a 64. We finished boot camp on June 12, 1943 and were all promoted to Seaman 2nd class. Shortly thereafter the USO put on a show in the Sullivan auditorium and featured the Jenkins Troupe.

The Sampson News reported the following: "Comedian Allen Jenkins and Betty Garrett, one of the featured singers in the New York stage hit, 'Something For The Boys' are shown on the stage of Sullivan auditorium where they presented a smart show last Sunday night for Sampson Bluejackets. Jenkins brought a dozen members of his cast of the Broadway show, including Billy Lynn, to the station under USO Camp Shows Sponsorship. In the smashing finale, girls of the chorus line brought recruits up on the stage to sing them a special sailor's song." In the official US Navy photograph I was pictured dancing with one of the showgirls. That was a great night.

Following this, we all went home for one week of boot leave. Although it was nice to be home, I was ready to get back because my buddies were all away and my brother Raymond was enlisted in the Army.

I returned to Sampson Naval Training Station where I was placed in the Outgoing Unit and became friends with a fellow by the name of Jack Whitehead. He was from the Allentown area and I never saw him again after we left the unit. I often wondered what happened to him.

There wasn't much to do while we awaited our transfers. They posted lists on bulletin boards twice a day that featured the names of fellows being transferred out. It must have really affected the fellows to not know what was going to happen to them because one of them was found out by railroad track. He had placed his head on the track as a train went by.

16

Key West Fleet Sound School

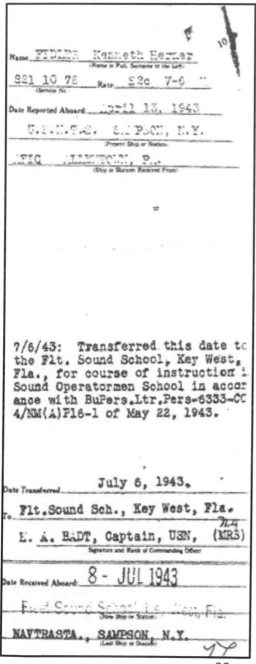

Name FIELDS Kenneth Homer

821 10 78 Rate S2c 7-6

Date Reported Aboard April 13, 1943

U.S.N.T.S. SAMPSON, N.Y.

NTC NEWPORT, R.I.

7/6/43: Transferred this date to the Flt. Sound School, Key West, Fla., for course of instruction i Sound Operatormen School in accor ance with BuPers.Ltr.Pers-6333-CC 4/NM(A)P16-1 of May 22, 1943.

Date Transferred July 6, 1943.

To Flt.Sound Sch., Key West, Fla.

E. A. BADT, Captain, USN, (MRS)

Date Received Aboard 8 - JUL 1943

Fleet Sound School Key West, Fla.

NAVTRASTA., SAMPSON, N.Y.

Finally, on July 6, I received my orders to transfer to Fleet Sound School located in Key West, Florida and a small group of us left the next day by train. We wore our white uniforms and rode in day coaches. We didn't go by Pullman (sleepers) but we rode all night and of course there was no air conditioning. So, most of the fellows had their windows open and when we arrived in Miami the next morning our uniforms were anything but white. I guess I didn't mention that the train was pulled by a steam engine that burned soft coal and made a lot of smoke and soot.

Upon our arrival we were loaded onto buses and driven the rest of the way to Key West, arriving the afternoon of July 8, 1943. We were immediately assigned to a barracks and had a chance to bathe and put on clean clothes and it sure felt good. I was happy to arrive in Key West and to find out the barracks were much nicer than in boot camp. We were given time to settle in and look the place over and then a day or so later we were assigned to Sonar classes.

We were told it was a five week course and those who survived would be promoted to third class Sonarman. We spent the first two weeks in the class room learning the theory involved with making the equipment work and what it was supposed to do and why. When I first went into the Navy I was given a chance to list the kind of job I was interested in. I mentioned I had taken machine shop in high school and that I played a cello in the orchestra. I guess they figured I had a good ear because I was selected to attend Sonar School. There I met Jerry Fink and we became friends as soon as we found out we shared the same home state. He was from Gradyville and I was from Reading.

Sonar consisted of electronic equipment in a room up on the bridge of the ship. The equipment was tied in with more electronic equipment down in the keel of the ship with a projector that could be raised or lowered through the bottom of the ship. When the projector was in the lowered position, we could send out sound waves by operating the equipment up on the bridge. We could set the projector on search mode to send out sound waves at a distance of 1,000, 2,000 or 5,000 yards. The projector consisted of a stainless steel plate with a lot of steel pins in the plate and when current was sent to these pins it caused the plate to set off a vibration, thus sending out a sound wave. We controlled the direction that the projector was facing so that we knew where the sound wave was going.

This way we could set up a search pattern, searching from the beam to the bow in 5 degree steps starting on one side of the ship and then back to the other. If the sound wave we sent hit any object, we heard an echo. We then looked at the screen to determine what direction and what distance it came from. If the echo had the same pitch it meant that the target was crossing our path. If the echo had a higher pitch, it meant the target was coming toward us. If the echo had a lower pitch, we knew the target was going away from us.

These sound waves were sent out from only one side of the projector because the backside of the projector was a receiver used to listen for propeller noises and other sounds that we were trained to recognize. We learned these things in the first two weeks of training and as we got to understand this a little bit better, they put us on what they called attack teachers. This turned out to be sonar equipment that worked just like the real thing, except we were inside a building and we sent out sound waves and searched for submarines just as if we were at sea. If we heard an echo we reported it and went through the whole procedure and actually made a dummy attack. We were given a grade on every attack and had to do it over and over until we got it right.

We also operated another piece of equipment called the sonar stack. It stood about five feet high and we sat in front of it so that we were able to look at the compass that indicated the direction the projector was pointed. In the lower right hand corner below the compass was a hand wheel about eight inches in diameter. We sat there with our hands on the hand wheel and moved the projector in five degree steps. We started at the beam and moved forward until we reached the bow which was dead ahead. Then we went to the opposite beam and repeated the process. Each time a sound wave went out we moved the projector. So, if we were on the 1,000 yard scale we moved the projector twice as fast as if we were on the 2,000 yard scale. The longer the sound wave was sent out the more time there was between pings. This is why all Sonarmen are called Ping Jockeys.

We also learned how to use a chemical recorder. It was a piece of equipment that had a roll of paper in it that was treated with a special chemical and it was only turned on when we reported a contact which indicated that we were getting an echo. When the recorder was turned on, the roll of paper moved very slowly as a stylus moved back and forth across the paper in time with the sound wave that was sent out. If we got an echo back, the stylus sent out an electrical charge on the chemically treated paper making a little black dash. This black dash marked the distance the target was from the ship.

As we continued to get dashes and as the roll of paper kept moving and as the target got closer, the dashes kept moving to the left at a constant speed making a distinct line at an angle. From this we calculated the speed of the target and with other information we could figure its course and depth and whether or not it was a submarine.

Although we learned how to use the recorder, it was usually operated by the Sonar Officer. The Sonarman and the Sonar Officer made a team and when we picked up a target in actual combat they called "general quarters" which meant "all hands man your battle stations." The Sonar Officer manned the recorder while the Sonarman fed him the information. The Sonar Officer then told the Captain or the Officer of the Deck which way to steer and could also give the command to fire. Firing meant to roll depth charges over the stern or to shoot off hedgehogs or K guns. Hedgehogs were like small rockets (24 of them) that were fired in a pattern over the bow ahead of the ship and only exploded if they hit something solid.

K guns fired depth charges which were like big 50 gallon oil drums that were on two racks on the back of the ship. Each one was filled with high explosives and could be set to explode at whatever depth we wanted up to about 800 feet. We could roll them off the stern or fire them out the side with K guns which were located at both sides of the stern. Each gun held one depth charge and when fired the charge was sent out at a 45 degree angle and thrown out 50 yards from the side of the ship. We always had to make sure the ship was moving fast enough when we fired or rolled off the depth charges or we were in danger of sinking our own ship!

We spent the last three weeks of our training at sea. We were divided into groups of four or five and every day each group went out on a different ship. Some of the ships were what they called Sub Chasers. They were small ships about 125 to 150 feet long, but they had Sonar equipment, depth charges and hedgehogs on them. There were a couple of Patrol Craft which were larger than the Sub Chasers, maybe around 150 to 200 feet long. We trained on another ship called the Eagle boat. It was pretty new but it was top heavy and they poured cement in the keel so that it didn't roll over.

There were two or three old World War I submarines that went out with us to act as submerged enemies. It was our job to locate them and when we did we made a practice attack just like they were the real enemy. If we thought we had a good target and were fairly certain it was a submarine, we fired the hedgehogs from a distance of 200 to 300 yards.

A funny thing happened one day while we were out training at sea. We had been searching all afternoon with our sonar equipment and all of a sudden we received a good sonar contact. We reported it to the Captain and made a practice run on it. Well, everything seemed to be going along fine and all of a sudden one of our submarines surfaced in the opposite direction and sent us a message, "What are you doing over there? We are over here!" As it turned out, this particular day there was only one friendly submarine out with us and that was the one that just surfaced. So, what were we chasing?

After a while we determined that it definitely was a submarine so it had to be the enemy. About that time we lost contact with the sub and several other ships joined the search with us. Then, because it was getting late in the afternoon, and they were a little worried about us students being there, they decided to collect us from each ship and put us on the friendly submarine and send us all into shore. You can imagine our disappointment, but we had an interesting trip going back

41

in an old World War 1 sub. We found out later they regained contact with the sub and they think they damaged it but it gave them the slip.

At the end of five weeks of training at Fleet Sound School in Key West, I graduated 35th in a class of 65. My final mark was 81.75. We had to earn at least a 62.5 in order to pass.

On August 14, 1943, I was promoted from Seaman 2nd class to Soundman 3rd class. The name of this rate was later changed to Sonarman 3rd class and was equal to a Buck Sergeant in the Army.

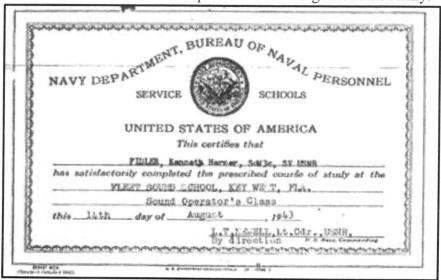

17

USS Loy DE 160 Norfolk, VA.

On August 17, 1943, I received orders to report to the Naval Operating Base in Norfolk, Virginia for further transfer to the USS Loy DE 160. I was due to report aboard August 21 but the Loy was a brand new ship that was in her final stages of construction. Because of this all of us who were sent to Norfolk were temporarily housed in a barracks in St. Helena, Norfolk Naval Base.

Upon arriving on the Loy, we found out there were six Sonarmen assigned to the ship and we got four more a little later. We were all new and fresh out of school. Besides myself there was Carl Jerome Fink (Jerry) from Gradyville, PA, Raymand V. Eldridge from New Brunswick NJ, Winfred A. Friberg from Malden, MA, Gerald A. Gagnon, (home unknown), and J. C. Rider, (home unknown).

The other four fellows who arrived were Sam Mezzatesta from Belleville, NJ, Frank Meadows from Lake Worth, FL, a fellow by the name of Brown who came on with Frank Meadows but didn't stay on very long. There was one more Sonarman at this time but I can't seem to remember his name. Our division officer was Lieutenant Robert P. Haun, A.S.W. Officer which stood for Anti Submarine Warfare and he was from Lancaster, PA.

The USS Loy was scheduled for commissioning on September 12, 1943. The officers and men attached to the Navy Yard continued with training programs and became familiar with the ship as she emerged from the final stages of construction. This was a novel period to the vast majority of those who had never been aboard a ship. We spent every day on board with working parties familiarizing ourselves with the ship which was cluttered with civilian workers. There were a lot of painters, plumbers, welders, electricians and quite a few female construction workers. The ship was littered with cables, hoses and lines all over the place.

Some of our working parties helped load stores, or were sometimes assigned a fire watch, which meant we were given a fire extinguisher and sent to stand near a welder in case something caught fire. Often the welder was in one compartment while the fire watchman was in the next compartment on the opposite part of the bulkhead in case something got hot and started to burn.

43

While we were still living in the barracks the whole crew was given nice warm working jackets with the ship's name and our own name stenciled on it. I wore my jacket to fire watch and took it off because it was warm below deck. I hooked it on a bulkhead and later in the day I was sent to the next compartment. I left my jacket hanging on the bulkhead and realized at the end of the day that I couldn't find it. Then I realized they had spray painted the whole compartment and didn't bother to even move my jacket! There it was all covered with paint. Fortunately, I was able to get another jacket without too much trouble.

The physical aspects of our ship were designed in answer to frequent sinkings of merchantmen in the Atlantic. It was an inexpensive, quickly constructed, high speed, escort vessel capable of offensive operations against those forces of the enemy, which intruded upon our supply lanes in international commerce.

U. S. S. Loy
(DE 160)

Christening and Commissioning

Our ship was christened on September 12, 1943, and Commissioned the USS Loy DE 160 to commemorate the services of Jackson Keith Loy, Gunner's Mate Third class, USN. Loy was born in Effingham, IL on April 29, 1922 and was killed in action November 12, 1942. He first enlisted in Chicago on September 4, 1940 serving until his death. He received the Navy Cross posthumously with the following citation:

> *"For extraordinary heroism as a gunner aboard the U.S.S. San Francisco during action against enemy Japanese forces in the Solomon Islands area on November 12 and 13, 1942.*
>
> *Courageously refusing to abandon his gun in the face of an onrushing Japanese torpedo plane, Loy, with cool determination and utter disregard for his own personal safety, kept blazing away until the hostile craft plunged out of the sky in a flaming dive and crashed on his station. His grim perseverance and relentless devotion to duty in the face of certain death were in keeping with the highest traditions of the United States Naval Service. He gallantly gave up his life in the defense of his country."*

Following the usual difficulties associated with breaking a bottle of champagne on the ship's bow, the prospective commanding officer, his officers, the Commandant and assembled guests went aboard and were conducted aft for the commissioning ceremony. The Commandant ordered the ship placed in commission and delivered her to James V. Bewick of Annapolis, MD Lieutenant Commander, USN, who read his orders, assumed command and set the first watch.

I'll never forget the speech delivered by our new Captain Lieutenant Commander while we stood at attention on the fantail. Near the end of his speech he said, "I hope I will see the day that this ship goes down in history." I didn't like the way he said, "down"...I wasn't that great of a swimmer! By this time most of us were moved aboard ship and assigned bunks based on the division we were assigned to. I was in the O division, which consisted of Sonarmen, Radiomen, Electronic Technicians, Quartermasters and Signalmen. In other words, everyone who stood watch on the bridge was in the O division. In case you don't know where or what the bridge is on a ship, it is a deck, topside towards the forward part of the ship. From there the Captain, Officers or Pilot directed the ship with the help of the Quartermasters, Radiomen, Signalmen, and Sonarmen.

The O division and the 1st division slept in the mess hall, which was below the main deck in the forward part of the ship. My bunk happened to be right at the foot of a ladder, which everyone had to use to get down to the mess hall. The ladder was pretty steep and a little difficult to navigate in bad weather with the ship rolling back and forth. All the food for the mess hall was carried down the ladder from the galley. In really bad weather there was no telling what I would find in my shoes in the morning as they sat at the foot of the ladder by my bunk. One morning they were filled with sections of grapefruit.

Following the christening of the ship we gradually settled into our new home. It took quite a while to get used to finding my way around while living on a ship in such close quarters with 180 other men.

Roster of Enlisted Personnel, U. S. S. Lo

ABRAMOWITZ, I. S1c
ADAMS, T. K. S2c
ALEXANDER, J. R. WT1c
ANDERSON, A. A. S2c
ARMS, J. H. F2c
AUSTIN, J. B. MM2c
BAGLIVI, H. J. S2c
BALCH, E. F. CM2c
BALLARD, I. L. FC3c
BARROWS, G. W. EM3c
BEAVERS, R. E. S2c
BELLOWS, F. H. SM1c
BERNDT, K. A. S2c
BONSIGNORD, F. S1c
BOUZAS, K. A. TM3c
BOYD, R. L. F1c
BRADLEY, J. P. MM2c
BRIANO, E.E. F2c
BRILLENT, F. S. PhM1c
BUREN, H. R. WT1c
BUSH, J. W. F1c
BYRD, R. R. MM1c
CALNAN, D. M. MM2c
CARTER, G. M. S2c
CHANCE, M. R. TM3c
CHUKAYNE, E. C. S2c
COBB, V. S. S2c
COLCLOUGH, P. F2c
COLGAN, T. P. Cox
COMPTON, E. D. CEM(PA)
COOK, A. W. S2c
CRUTCHFIELD, R. L. S2c
CURRIER, R. E. S2c
DANIELSON, A. A. S1c
DAWSON, F. A. SC3c
DAVIS, J. V. S2c
DELANEY, P. J. Cox
DELOSE, R. F. RM3c
DOMBROWSKY, J. L. SC3c
ELDRIDGE, R. V. SoM3c
ELLITHORP, W. I. SF3c
ENTSMINGER, R. F. F2c
FIDLER, K. H. SoM3c
FINK, C. J. SoM3c
FINLEY, D. E. S2c
FOSTER, R. A. SC3c
FRIBERG, W. A. SoM3c
GADEBERG, F. A. EM1c
GAGNON, G. A. SoM3c
GARVIN, J. R. S2c
GODFREY, D. R. S2c
GREEN, J. H. S2c
GRIMES, J. J. MM2c
GROSS, G. M. S3c
GRUBER, J. F. S1c
HABERSTROH, H. J., Jr. F2c
HAGNAUT, C. C. S2c
HARRIS, J. M. S2c
HART, O. K. SoM2c
HEYOT, R. A. S2c
HIMEBROOK, C. CCS(PA)
HOFFMAN, J. W. F2c
HOYT, G. B. F2c
HUGGETT, J. W. F2c
ISAAC, E. L. S2c
JACOBS, C., Jr. F2c
JEFFORDS, C. O. S2c
JENKINS, H. B. S2c
JENSEN, R. H. F2c
JOHNSON, G. H. S2c
JOHNSON, R. E. GM1c
JONES, S2c
JONES, H. H. S2c
JONES, W. E. S2c
KARPAVAGE, J. S2c
KAY, J. C., Jr. S2c
KEELEY, R. C. S2c
KEITH, O. L. S2c
KELLEY, T. A. S2c
KENNEDY, H. C. S2c
KIBBLE, B. J. S2c
KIGER, K. N. S2c
KIRCHOFF, D. R. EM1c
KIRK, R. C. S2c
KIRK, J. H. GM2c
KLINE, A. L. S2c
KULIN, H. S. S2c
KUNTZ, C. M. S2c
LANGLEY, L. W. S7c
LATTY, H. A. S2c
LAWSON, H. A. S2c
LAXTON, F. W. S2c
LEAGAN, R. M. S2c
LEASE, R. A. S2c
LEE, D. E. S2c
LEE, E. E. S2c
LEO, E. F2c

LEROY, G. H. QM2c
LESSLIE, J. B. S2c
LEWIS, E. R. S2c
LINCOLN, R. R. S2c
LITTLE, H. K. S2c
LISS, M. S2c
LLOYD, W. H. MM2c
LOGAN, W. R. S2c
LONG, A., Jr. S2c
LONG, A. MM2c
LODIER, C. B. S2c
LOVE, D. M. S2c
LOWERY, E. J. S2c
LUMPKIN, J. W. S2c
LUNDY, J. E. S2c
LUNDY, J. M. RM2c
LUNSFORD, P. G. S2c
LUNSY, R. H., Jr. S2c
LYNCH, A. S. S2c
LYNCH, E. D. CMM(PA)
McBRIDE, M. S. S2c
McCLELLAN, W. S2c
McCLURG, C. S2c
McCOY, J. D. S2c
McGUIRE, P. M. F3c
McKNIGHT, J. M. QM3c
McRORIE, R. R. S2c
MACGUIGAN, T. L. S2c
MANOK, H. J. S2c
MARLOWE, E. R. S2c
MARR, W. R. S2c
MARTIN, C. F. S2c
MARTIN, D. L. S2c
MARTIN, H. S2c
MARTIN, J. R. F3c
MARTIN, M. M. S2c
MARTIN, M. R. S2c
MATHIAS, J. C. S2c
MATHIS, J. L. S2c
MATNEY, L. S2c
MATTOX, H. W. S2c
MAULDIN, O. J. S2c
MAY, E. R. S2c
MAY, H. E. S2c
MAYER, J. J. Y1c
MEDEIROS, J. S2c
MELITO, F. J. S2c
MELLO, A. S2c
MILES, W. W. Y2c
MILLIKIN, D. F3c
MINDISH, S. S2c
MOLENDA, J. J. S2c
MONTEITH, W. H. S2c
MONTGOMERY, J. E. F3c
MORANDI, A. CBM(AA)
MORGAN, E. A. CRM(PA)
MORRIS, W. H. S2c
NEMEC, A. M. F3c
NICHOLSON, J. C. EM3c
NORRIS, C. H. EM3c
O'LEARY, J. B. F3c
PECORARO, A. P. S2c
PHILLIPS, C. H. CWT(PA)
RAMSEY, F. D. S2c
REHM, R. FC3c
RIDER, J. C. SoM3c
RUCKDESCHEL, V. E. S2c
SANDS, C. L. S2c
SCARPELLI, F. F2c
SCHAUB, J. L. MM3c
SCHURLKNIGHT, D. E. SK3c
SEVERYNIAK, T. K. S2c
SHEPHARD, M. B. GM3c
SIMS, C. C. F3c
SMITH, L. D. F3c
SMITH, R. J. F1c
SNODGRASS, P. L. F3c
TAYLOR, O. E. S2c
TAYLOR, R. L. Ck3c
TEFFT, M. W. F3c
TOLBERT, J. J. S2c
USKEVICH, S. B. S2c
VOIGT, E. C. EM3c
WALKER, T. C. SoM2c
WEAVER, R. H. PhM2c
WELCH, E. V. MM2c
WESTERMAN, A. L. S2c
WHITNEY, R. F3c
WINTERS, H. A. S2c
WINTERSTEEN, R. C. S2c
WISE, C. S2c
WISE, H. R. F3c
WOODALL, E. M. RM3c
WOODARD, F. StM2c
WOODARD, R. L. StM2c
WOODHOUSE, H. K. RT1c
WOLLARD, M. N. M2c
WRIGHT, H. S2c

18

Bermuda

The ship continued fitting out and receiving supplies, then finally went out to sea on her maiden voyage. You have to realize that about 85% of us had never seen the ocean, let alone been on a ship before. Our crew formed around a small nucleus of experienced trained veterans from other ships, even from some ships that had been sunk. It didn't take long to be able to tell the difference between them and the rest of us.

Our maiden voyage, better known as our shakedown cruise turned out to be a winner. We left Norfolk about the middle of October 1943, heading for Bermuda. The first night out we ran into a bad hurricane off of Cape Hatteras, a place known for terrible storms. Just about everyone got seasick on our first night at sea. Most of us were supposed to stand watch four hours on and eight hours off. Well, most of us did but we nearly died doing it. I think it took us three or four days to get to Bermuda, and the weather was so bad they couldn't do much cooking.

One day they tried to make soup in the big kettles shaped like drums. However, when they filled them, half of the soup ran out because the ship was rolling so much. Just picture this: The mess hall was below the main deck and the cooks had to carry food down steep ladders while the ship was rolling back and forth 30 to 40 degrees. At the same time we were pitching up and down like we were on an elevator...it was almost an impossible job and the food was in sad shape by the time they got it to the mess hall. As you can imagine, there were not too many sailors interested in eating by then.

The mess hall consisted of tables welded to the deck big enough to seat about five or six men on each side. The only trouble was the benches weren't fastened to the deck. They had collapsible legs on each end and that is just what they did...collapse. If we were lucky enough to feel like eating and were able to get a tray of food to a table without falling on the slippery deck, we had to try to sit on the bench and hold on to the table to keep from sliding away while trying to eat!

At the same time the ship was rolling back and forth and if we didn't lift our trays up to match the angle we pitched at, the food ran out onto our laps. If we lifted the tray we had to hold onto something on the table or we slid away from the table along with everyone else on our bench. One of the fellows sitting on the end of a bench accidentally got his leg under the bench too far. He knocked the hook that held the leg in place and the whole bench collapsed with everyone on it! I guess you can understand when I say there weren't too many meals served on the way to Bermuda. Most of us didn't feel much like eating and those who did survived mostly on graham crackers, fruit and coffee. It was the small group of experienced veterans who ran the ship that first night or two. The rest of us were at our watch station when we had to be, but most of the time we had our heads in a bucket. It was awful!

By the time we reached Bermuda the storm let up or we were getting our sea legs. Either way, it sure felt good to get back in port again. Before we were able to go ashore, we had a big job of cleaning the entire ship. The storm was bad enough but with everyone being seasick the ship was a real mess. Our most vivid recollection of this period was the struggle we encountered in acquiring sea legs, rough seas, general seasickness, work and lack of sleep. Compensations such as liberty were scarce, but by the end of October each man had been ashore once before we departed.

19

New York-Aruba-Bizerte Convoy Duty

We returned to the Norfolk Navy Yard for five days where we made final adjustments and tests. Then we proceeded to New York to report for duty, and Boston was our designated homeport. A Destroyer Escort Division was formed and our first orders directed us to sail on November 12 to North African ports via Aruba Dutch West Indies and to return to New York via Aruba as routed by Admiralty. Naturally, we were pleased with this duty because it kept us in the warm and calm waters of the South Atlantic. Eventually we returned to New York at the Admiralty's pleasure.

Looking back, I remember a few of the discomforts we encountered. There always seemed to be a shortage of fresh water while under way to Bermuda and Aruba. Those responsible for operating the equipment to make the fresh water couldn't seem to keep it running enough to keep us supplied. Because of this, the drinking fountains were available at certain times of the day and when we showered we used salt-water soap. When they did let us shower with fresh water, there was someone standing right there to make sure we turned off the water after getting wet and to ensure we didn't turn it back on until we were soaped up and ready to rinse.

By the time we reached Aruba, we were still having fresh water problems so we decided to get water from one of the tankers. They filled up our water tanks from a tanker. Later we found out Aruba also had a shortage of water. A lot of the tankers we escorted down to Aruba from New York had filled their tanks with water to bring down to Aruba. They left the water in Aruba and then filled the same tanks with oil they took to Africa. When they got back to New York, they filled the same tanks with water to take back down to Aruba. The trouble was the water we got from the tanker tasted awful after being stored in an oil tank. The water was used to make coffee, tea, powdered milk, and soup, and that made them all taste bad. Like everything else, we eventually got used to it until they decided to paint the water tanks. That made the water taste terrible again!

Our first crossing took us to Bizerte, French Tunisia, North Africa. In Aruba we picked up a large convoy of freighters and tankers and started out in the direction of North Africa. The convoy consisted of 100 ships positioned 10 in a row and 10 rows. We were one of about 12 destroyer escorts and our stations were out in front of the convoy and part way down each side. A couple escorts also patrolled the rear. Since we had so many Sonarmen on the ship, we were assigned other duties as well. They were short of Radarmen so they trained some of us to operate radar and set up a watch where we rotated every hour or so between radar, sonar and bridge talker. That really made it much nicer and not quite so boring.

Bridge talkers were up on the open bridge with the Officer of the Deck. We had a headset so we were in communications with all the gun crews and everyone else who was on watch at the time, including the lookouts. It was real interesting being right where all the action was unfolding and many times we found out what was happening ahead of time. Of course a lot of the time the Captain was right there, so we had to keep out of his way and not make any mistakes.

Standing radar watch meant being in a room right under the open bridge called the Combat Information Center, where the radar equipment was housed. It also housed a big plotting board used to plot course and speeds of targets reported from the radar or sonar. There was also some radio equipment and radio directional equipment used for navigation. We stood Sonar watch in the Sonar Shack. It was located in a room in the forward part of the open bridge. The Captain's chair on the open bridge was right outside the Sonar shack entrance, so we had to behave ourselves.

Normally, the ships in the convoy maintained a certain course and speed. The job of the escorts was to protect the convoy from submarines. Each escort was assigned a certain station to protect and usually zig zagged back and forth while searching for submarines. In other words the main convoy was on a straight course while the escorts zigzagged back and forth. If an escort picked up what they thought to be a submarine contact, a signal was passed to all ships in the convoy to turn 90 degrees at a given command to get out of harm's way. This was done by signal light or flag signal and on rare occasions the radio was used. We avoided this as much as possible because the goal was to maintain radio silence. When the convoy was given the signal to turn, 100 big ships turned at the same time and it was quite a sight to see.

The convoy could only go as fast as the slowest ship, which was only about 6 knots or 166 miles in 24 hours unless the winds and tides were with us; then we could do more. Unfortunately, both were against us and some days we did as little as 100 miles. That gave us quite an uncomfortable feeling when we knew enemy submarines were lurking around.

I stood watch a lot with Radarman Paul G. Lunsford from Cambridge City, IN. He was almost 20 years older than I was and seemed like an old man at the time even though he was only about 38 years old. He always had a chew in his mouth but we got along real well. I guess he was like a father image to me. I always hoped to see him at one of the reunions, but I found out he passed away December 3, 1987.

Howard J. Manor from Grand Rapids, OH and Moe Liss from New York were other fellows I got to know by standing watch with them. Moe loved to play poker and shoot craps. I think he sent a lot more money home from gambling than he earned from the Navy. He was troubled with chronic seasickness, although most fellows thought he was putting on. As soon as they pulled up the anchor he had his bucket with him and he got sick. Having stood a lot of watches with him, I'm pretty sure he was not putting on. He eventually transferred off the ship and got shore duty.

Once in a while bad weather slowed us down to a standstill. The worst time was at night. We had ten rows of ships and ten in a row that had to stay close enough to the ship in front so as to be able to stay in a straight line. All escorts had radar, but a lot of the convoy ships had none. This meant that at night they had to be able to see the ship in front of them, which was especially tough in fog, rain, or even just a pitch black night. No ship was allowed to show any light at night because that was a good way to get sunk, and the nearest land was straight down!

We escorts used our radar to keep a close eye on the convoy at night. If we saw a ship getting out of line or falling back too far, one of us escorts was sent into the convoy, up between the lines of ships until we were close enough to yell at them with a bull horn to move it up or get back in line or to find out what the trouble was. We always hated that job because there was the danger of collision. This usually happened in the middle of the night when most of the crew was sleeping so it was not a job any of us looked forward to.

Besides standing our regular watch of four hours on and eight hours off during the day, we worked around the ship on the eight hours off. Working hours were from 8:00 AM to 4:30 PM and if you weren't on watch during those hours you worked. We kept cleaning stations clean and we ended up painting a lot of the time. We painted all the way across the Atlantic and when we got close to Africa we either threw what paint we had left over the side or gave it to a passing ship headed home. The paint was too dangerous to keep onboard because it was a fire hazard.

The standing rule was to have enough fuel to be able to reach land. When we got close to not having enough then we pulled up alongside a tanker to refuel. This meant running alongside the tanker and throwing lines over to them so they could send a hose back and then pump oil into our tanks while we steamed along like nothing was happening. As the ship's fuel tanks ran empty they were filled with water to maintain the ballast so we didn't roll all over the place. So, all the tanks of water were pumped out right before we went alongside the tanker to refuel.

As we approached North Africa we tried to plan it to pass through the straits of Gibraltar at night. That way we weren't seen from lookouts on shore. Many of us will never forget we were told there was a big convoy a couple days ahead of us going through the Mediterranean. They were attacked by a bunch of German airplanes and evidently some of the ships were sunk because we began to see the effects of it. There was a new moon out and it just threw enough light on the water to make it quite eerie looking. After a while we started to see bodies floating by along with a lot of debris. This went on half the night and we got our first bitter taste of war.

After 21 long days, we finally reached Bizerte, French Tunisia, North Africa. We saw a lot of sunken ships in the harbor but after a while our ship was allowed to make our way in and tie up at a dock. It was nice to finally get ashore. We were told they had just secured the area and saw a lot of prisoners of war being marched away. I believe they were mostly Italian. The American soldiers were surprised to see us and said we were the first warship of our size to arrive, and we weren't even that big.

We were allowed to go ashore in our dungarees and one evening found out the Army was going to show a movie in one of the Quonset huts. Some of us managed to get there at the right time. As we waited for the movie to start, in walked General Bradley and some of his staff. That was exciting!

On December 17, we left Bizerte for our return trip home. As promised, we bummed paint from the first ships we ran across while traveling through the straits of Gibraltar. We painted our way back across the Atlantic and the trip home seemed to be going pretty good. The winds and tide were behind us and we made really good time. We were supposed to take the convoy back to Aruba and then all the escorts were to go back to New York so everyone would get leave to go home. However, we weren't quite that lucky.

We found ourselves midway across the Atlantic on Christmas day and one of the ships in the convoy broke down with boiler trouble. We were ordered to remain with her. So not only were we midway across the Atlantic, we patrolled a circle 2,000 yards in radius around the crippled merchantman as well. If that wasn't bad enough, we also received word there were three sightings of German submarines in our area. Fortunately, we never saw any of them. Repairs were soon made to the ship and we proceeded. We got back to Aruba in time to find out the rest of our division had already left for New York and we were to stay until they returned for the next trip. You can imagine how that went over with everyone.

20

Curacao-Guantanamo Bay

After this fiasco they decided to let us go to Curacao for a little rest and recreation. It was the largest island in the Netherlands Antilles and it was absolutely beautiful. As we entered the bay and sailed almost right into the town, we noticed the houses were painted all different colors. The name of the town was Willemstad and it was the capital of the Netherlands Antilles where most of the people spoke Dutch, English, and Spanish. We stayed there only a few days before we were sent to the Naval Base at Guantanamo Bay, Cuba for refresher training and upkeep in preparation for another trip to Africa.

Most of the training we received was mainly for Officers and Sonarmen, of which I was one. We were sent to a base building with what they called attack teachers. This was equipment similar to what we used at Key West Sonar School. They wanted us to freshen up our attack procedures in case we ran into any submarines on our next trip. We were there only a few days, then got underway headed for Aruba where we picked up another 100 ship convoy.

On January 14, 1944 we sailed a similar voyage, this time stopping at Algiers, North Africa. We had some pretty rough sailing weather and a few scares with German submarines, but otherwise it was pretty much like the other trip. Enemy aircraft hit the convoy a few days ahead of us pretty hard. Again, we were very fortunate. It was a little different stopping at Algiers instead of Bizerte. Algiers was a big port and we were allowed to go on liberty, but we were warned it was pretty dangerous to go alone and that we should go in pairs or small groups. We heard about a lot of sailors traveling alone who were beaten or robbed.

We also discovered that the Arabs seemed to have a lot of money and wanted to buy wristwatches, jewelry, cigarettes and anything else we had to sell. I had an old wrist watch with a broken crystal. It didn't run anymore, but when I saw what they were buying I shook it until it started running and quickly sold it for $40. I found out they were interested in the jeweled movement inside the watch. Some of the fellows sold their mattress covers for $20, which was equal to a new suit of clothes for the Arabs.

One fellow came back aboard ship in his under shorts and we thought he had been robbed. It turned out he sold everything he had on but his shorts! We stayed in Algiers for one week and it was there our commanding officer was detached from the ship and his executive officer, Robert W. Pond of Boston, MA, Lieutenant Commander USNR, succeeded in command. A short ceremony was held on the fantail and after wishing us happy hunting, Captain Bewick departed with the hope, "We would all meet again."

Several days following our departure and beyond the Rock of Gibraltar, we received orders to proceed to the Brooklyn Navy Yard after the delivery of our convoy to Aruba. The news was passed over the ship's public address system, and the response was no less in volume than a home run scored by our favorite baseball team. We arrived in Aruba on the February 20, 1943.

21

Leave

We arrived in New York the latter part of February and each man was granted six days leave. They split the crew into port and starboard sections; half went home for six days and the other half went when the first half returned. I think that is when I first met Bill Morris, even though we had both been on the ship since the commissioning. We happened to get on the same train from New York to Philadelphia and eventually ended up on the same train going to Reading. We talked all the way and got to know each other. He was going to visit his brother in Pottstown, and before he left we made arrangements to go back to the ship on the same train.

It was nice to get back home to Reading and be with my mother even though all my friends were in the service and my brother was in the Army. However, it wasn't long until I was ready to go back and get it over with. After we went back to the ship we got a chance to see a lot of New York because we were able to get liberty almost every night.

On one of these nights, Bill Morris met his girlfriend Marge and they were eventually married. The day after he met Marge, I went on a blind date with him and Marge and Marge's girlfriend who worked with her at Western Union. Her name was Emily Schultz. We dated after that and corresponded for a long time.

22

Casco-Bay-Boston

As soon as the work was completed in the Navy yard we were ordered to proceed to Casco Bay, ME. We spent more time using sonar attack teachers in Portland and exercises at sea with other ships where we became very familiar with the shores of Maine. From Casco Bay we proceeded to Boston but our visit and liberty there was cut short because of orders we received to join a huge troop convoy headed for England. However, we broke off near Halifax when a New York section joined up to replace us. We returned to Casco Bay March 26 for further training coordinated with battleship maneuvers in preparation for the Normandy Invasion. Not until later did we realize the import of our exercises.

23

Hunter Killer Mission

On March 30th, we departed for Norfolk and were ordered to escort one of the light aircraft carriers in a hunter killer mission against submarines reputedly concentrated in the North Atlantic. Our additional duties were to clear the lanes and protect the convoy crossing the South Atlantic to which the other ships in our division were assigned. We headed out to sea April 3, 1944 sailing with the light aircraft carrier USS Core CVE 13. She was a small aircraft carrier converted from a merchant ship and was a lot shorter than the regular aircraft carriers. This made it a little harder for an airplane to land on, especially in rough weather when the carrier's bow bobbed up and down in the big waves.

The carrier assigned the USS Loy to get into tail back position, which meant that when the carrier got into position to receive landing airplanes or to launch aircraft, we were supposed to go to the stern of the carrier and follow as close as possible in case a plane crashed into the water and needed our assistance. The carrier set sail the first day with most of her planes still on shore bases. Around noon her aircraft started arriving and the carrier moved into position to receive the planes.

To accept her aircraft, she had to go into the wind as fast as she could go. The Loy took her position at tailback and the planes began landing. Everything went fine until the end. One of the planes came in following too close to the plane ahead of it and was waved off and told to make a big circle and try again. However, instead of making a big circle, he made a tight small circle and lost too much speed and side slipped until his wing hit the water with one big splash and he was gone. Even though we were close to the plane, all we found was a wheel. I guess that pilot was a little too sure of himself. We found out later he was an air ace with quite a few enemy planes to his credit.

At the outset our duty was bounded by the geographic generalities of the North and South Atlantic. The duty actually encompassed these directions and all the space between and we were at sea from April 3 to April 29. During this period we traveled in the roughest water the ship ever sailed where rolls of 65 degrees were not uncommon.

I think there were about four or five of us destroyer escorts with the carrier in the hunter killer group. While we were in the Brooklyn Navy Yard, all of us destroyer escorts had a new type of radio direction finder installed. A very long antenna was attached to the top of our mast and new radio equipment was installed in the CIC room with a between-ships voice radio next to it. The radio equipment was a special high frequency unit that was used to listen for German submarines when they surfaced at night to broadcast back to Berlin.

The equipment was called HFDF, which stood for High Frequency Direction Finder. The radio had an operator on it 24 hours a day and each ship in our group was assigned a different station to listen to. Each station had a code name and if one ship heard a submarine broadcasting on the station it was guarding, the operator immediately picked up the telephone between ships and said the code name of the station so all the other ships would change to that station and try to get a bearing on the submarine with their direction finder. Then they took those bearings from each ship and located the submarines where the lines intersected. That got pretty exciting sometimes.

When I stood watch at sea, I was either in the Sonar Shack standing Sonar watch; on the open bridge with an officer employed as a bridge talker or I stood Radar watch in the Combat Information Center (CIC). I always worked with an experienced radar operator while standing watch in the CIC and that is how we Sonarmen learned all about radar. Also, it was necessary to have two people working together in case we picked up a target on the radar. That way one of us did the tracking on the plotting board to figure out the target's course and speed. There were also Radiomen with us in the CIC who guarded the radio frequency of the HFDF equipment in case a German submarine started to broadcast to Berlin. It wasn't unusual for a German sub to surface late at night to get fresh air and to charge their batteries and at the same time send a message back to Berlin. The messages were anything from weather reports, fuel reports, to reporting the sinking of enemy ships.

The carrier usually sent up aircraft every day on reconnaissance missions over large areas of the ocean looking for submarines and German Raiders. These were good-sized ships flying a flag of a neutral country and looking harmless. However, when we went up close to investigate or asked permission to come aboard, the sides of the ship suddenly fell away and we'd be looking at a row of big guns pointing right at us. Then they ran up the German flag and we had to be ready to fight back or else we are in BIG trouble.

The aircraft carried something called sonar buoys. In fact they carried a bunch of the little radio receivers that allowed them to see submerged submarines on a clear day when the water was calm. Sometimes they dropped at least four of these sonar buoys at a time and the one coming in the clearest or loudest indicated the direction of the submarine. Even if the pilot couldn't see submarines in the water but had a report of a sub sighting, he dropped a bunch of these in the water and possibly pick up the sounds of the submarine propellers.

After determining the submarine's direction, he either dropped depth charges on it or reported it to the carrier, which sent one or two destroyer escorts to the area and try to sink it. To do this they used either hedgehogs or depth charges. It was a standing rule, though, if the sub surfaced and tried to fight it out, our Captain was ordered to ram the sub, even if it meant the destroyer escort going down with it. They said it was worth it, but I think it's easier to believe that if you're not on one!

As I said earlier, we always had to have enough fuel to reach land. We were somewhere off the coast of France when we needed to get fuel from the carrier. We tried but the sea was very rough with high winds, and we couldn't get close enough to safely refuel. We decided to wait a day or so to see if the weather improved, but it got worse. We waited another day or so for things to calm down.

In the meantime, we had to fill our empty tanks with water for ballast so we wouldn't have trouble controlling the ship while bobbing around like a cork. Finally our tanks ran dangerously low and we decided to give it one more try even though the weather was terrible. First, we pumped out all the water, which meant we rode high in the water as we proceeded with caution up alongside of the carrier. We rolled back and forth pretty badly, but managed to shoot a line over, which they fastened to a hose and our men pulled the hose over to our ship. The hose was secured to the opening of the fuel hatch and we started to pump oil. It isn't easy for two ships to ride side by side at an even pace and with high waves and strong wind, it is just about impossible.

The carrier was much bigger than the Loy. Her main deck was 40 feet off the water. The Loy, whose main deck was 3 to 4 feet above the water, had a 90 foot mast swinging side to side like an upside down pendulum. As any ship cuts through the water it makes wey or in other words the waves come down each side of the ship at about a 45 degree angle. If the ship gets inside those waves she is pushed in closer to the carrier. That is what our ship had to contend with and soon after they started pumping oil our ship got inside those waves. We were pushed in closer to the carrier until our mast started pounding on the carrier's main deck 40 feet above us.

As our helmsman tried to give more right rudder to get away from the carrier, our fantail (stern), which is only 3 to 4 feet above the water, slid in against the carrier just as the stern of the carrier rose from the heavy waves. When the carrier's stern came back down, it landed right on top of our fantail, smashing the K guns which carried depth charges. Our Captain remained calm and collected and gave the order to cut all lines and stop all engines. The carrier slowly pulled away from us without any more damage, although one of our men either fell over the side or jumped. I wish I remembered if we pulled him to safety or not.

We also quickly dropped the two damaged depth charges over the side after making sure they were set on "safe." No one could figure out why they never blew up when the carrier smashed them and we were happy they didn't. If they had blown up they would have taken the carrier and us with it. We considered ourselves lucky again.

After that, the project was abandoned in favor of a short detachment to the smoother waters of the Azores. Evidently, before we had to disconnect they were able to pump enough fuel into our tanks to get us to the Azores. There was only one hitch in meeting our destination. The Azores was neutral, which meant we might tie up next to a German submarine. That wasn't so bad but as we arrived or left the Azores, the German sub could be out there waiting for us. Fortunately, we were able to enter the harbor, fill our tanks, and get out of there in a short time. Since it was a neutral country we had to be out of there in less than 24 hours or the government could intern us until the end of the war. As soon as we left the Azores we proceeded to rejoin the hunter killer group.

The day after we were back with the carrier, we sighted a merchantman traveling independently and we were ordered to investigate. Naturally, we thought right away it could be a German Raider. On our approach all hands manned their battle stations, guns were trained on the target and a visit and search party proceeded with its mission. Following the inspection and anxious moments, the ship proved to be of Spanish registry and was allowed to proceed.

On April 29, we tied up at Casablanca, North Africa, but with our familiarity with North African ports we found nothing uncommon in our short visit which concluded on May 3. We departed with the carrier to continue our mission which ended with our arrival in New York in June. The departure from convoy escort duty will long be remembered for many reasons other than weather and the sea. We were one of five escorts and high speed frequent course changes necessitated screen reorientation, which posed the ever present unwelcome possibility of escorts converging on each other. Also, we will always marvel at the ability of the fliers to land and take off in total darkness from which even the frequent crack-ups could not detract.

We also found out later how lucky we really were. We had been with the USS Core CVE 13 those last couple months, but at the same time there had been another hunter killer group operating out there as well. The name of that carrier was the USS Block Island CVE 12 with five other destroyer escorts. It turned out they were not quite as lucky as we were. A torpedo sank the Block Island. Fortunately, most of her aircraft were in the air at the time. Some of the aircraft were able to make it to land safely, but many of them ran out of fuel and crashed into the sea or the pilot parachuted into the water to be picked up by a friendly ship.

One of the destroyer escorts managed to pick up the German sub on its sonar and made a couple attacks on it. They must have damaged the sub because it surfaced and tried to use deck guns against the escort. The escort tried to ram the sub. A big wave lifted them up and sent their bow up and over the sub where it lodged. A short hand-to-hand battle ensued but the crew of the escort managed to gain the upper hand and captured the sub. When we heard this, we realized how lucky we were.

Then we found out some other news. When we were assigned to go with the hunter killer operation, the destroyer USS Fetchler took our place with a convoy going to the Mediterranean. When that convoy got to the Mediterranean they were hit hard by German planes and the ship that took our place, the USS Fetchler, was sunk. After that we were called the "Lucky Loy."

Dear Sam:

Enclosed is a poem I wrote about the USS LANING (DE-159) and the heroic rescue they made on May 5, 1944 of 186 survivors of the USS FECHTELER (DE-157).

I would like to have it printed in the DESA News when it is convenient. The Laning had orders to forget the Fechteler crew in the water because the Submarine was still there. But without concern for their own lives they stopped their ship dead in the water and took on over 100 survivors. The crew of the Fechteler owe them our lives.

It was men like E. Arthur Shuman Jr. and his brave crew that made me proud to be part of the Destroyer Escort Navy. So anyone of the Laning crew that reads this poem, it comes from the bottom of my heart.

Curtis W. Toombs MM2/c
USS FECHTELER (DE-157)

A Tribute to the Laning

To E. Arthur Shuman and his brave crew
I owe them my life, I think we all do
They stopped their ship, dropped a raft
Picked up survivors both fore and aft.

They got all the survivors they could find
Made several runs leaving no one behind
They gave us dry clothing, put us to bed
Took care of our wounded, buried our dead.

Our longevity, the reunion we're planning
Would not be possible if not for the Laning
So E. Arthur Shuman where ever you may be
Thanks for pulling all of us out of the sea.

Curtis Toombs
Ashland, Ky.

24

New York- Bizerte

Following the customary twelve day availability in the Brooklyn Navy Yard with leave and liberty, we departed June 13. Our job included escorting a British carrier until we joined one of the huge convoys out of Norfolk that shuttled back and forth from the States to Africa with train-schedule regularity. Those convoys averaged about 85 ships each with 13 destroyer escorts, and undoubtedly, were the major channel of supply for the forces invading North Africa and Italy.

Between June and October, we made three crossings in the convoy lane between Norfolk and North Africa which averaged about 17 days and Bizerte was our only stop. On the way over we practiced every imaginable drill and the ship was prepared for an inspection in Bizerte twice and upon every visit to the States at both Brooklyn and Casco Bay. I remember the first of these three crossings. As we approached Bizerte, the Commodore of the convoy sent a message to our Captain, "Since you have been here before, your ship can lead the way." The harbor was full of sunken ships and Lord knows what all, but we started to lead the way and all of a sudden we ran aground. Then we got another message from the Commodore, "Never mind, we will find our own way." Well, you can imagine our Captain was fit to be tied. It was rather embarrassing, but he finally got the ship going without any other help.

Our stay was cut short in Bizerte and the Loy was ordered to escort a merchant ship through the Mediterranean as far as Gibraltar. As soon as we got underway, our Captain sent a message to the merchant ship that he wanted them to run at 15 knots and we zig zagged back and forth in front of them until we reached Gibraltar at night when traveling was safer. After a few hours the merchant ship slowed down to about six knots. We received a message from them saying they were having labor difficulties and that was as fast as they could go. Civilians ran the merchant ships and most of them had unions. We sailed all day and all night and we still weren't near Gibraltar.

The early morning weather was frigid as we passed Algiers and noticed a convoy passing us going the opposite direction. All of a sudden a British destroyer from the convoy got torpedoed and sank into the icy waters in no time at all. A few minutes later, our Captain received a message from the merchant ship. It stated, "Proceeding at 18 knots immediately." Evidently they got their labor difficulties straightened out in a hurry.

On another trip to Bizerte, I had the mid-watch which was midnight to 4:00 AM. I worked with an Ensign by the name of J. Marcus. About 2:00 AM Mr. Marcus said to me, "I am going to take a turn about the deck to see if I can catch anyone sleeping." Well, as soon as he left the bridge, I got on the headphones, which were connected with all the lookouts and gun crews and said, "Be on your toes, the OD is coming." Soon after that Mr. Marcus returned to the bridge and he was hopping mad. Right away he accused me of telling everyone he was coming and I said, "Who me?" I was charged with "Working against the best interests of the ship," and I had to go before the Captain while he listened to the charges. When I told him what I did, he restricted me to no liberty in the next port. It turned out that we pulled into some island to refuel for a few hours and that took care of my restriction.

The last time we were there, we had a chance to go on liberty into the town of Tunis. When I was a little boy I used to hear about this gangster who was head of the underworld in Reading. His name was Tony Moran. I heard he was from the town of Tunis, Tunisia, and I used to see his fancy car parked on Penn Street. It was a Chord, and I guess at the time I thought it was a big deal to be able to go to the town he was from.

We rode to town in an open stake body truck on a bumpy dirt road. It was quite a few miles to get there and when we arrived it wasn't great anyway. The town was badly damaged from the war and we couldn't find anything like a restaurant to get something to eat. Eventually another fellow and I found someone who sold us a couple hard-boiled eggs for 25 cents apiece. That liberty turned out to be a big fizzle.

We ran into some real bad weather as we traveled back to the States. We experienced rough seas for several days and then someone happened to notice the HFDF antenna up on top of the mast was coming loose and moving back and forth. The antenna was big and heavy, at least 20 feet long and was fastened to the top of the mast with a flange with a bunch of screws holding it together. Due to the rough seas, we were making 45 degree rolls each direction and the Captain was worried the antenna might come loose altogether and fall down and kill someone or damage the ship. He asked for a volunteer to climb up and try to tighten it, but it certainly wasn't easy because the ship was rolling so much. As an incentive he said he would give the volunteer double leave when we got into port. In other words, if we got seven days leave, he would give the volunteer fourteen days leave. A Radarman by the name of H. Kenneth Little volunteered to do the job and he did it successfully. He did, however, get quite a ride when he was up 90 feet at the top of the mast.

We were detached from convoying upon our return to the States in October. We proceeded independently from Norfolk to Boston for conversion in the South Boston Navy Yard where the USS Loy would be converted to an Auxiliary Personnel Destroyer. We tied up on October 8, 1944 and between then and December we became acquainted with our new home port which now had acquired a real meaning.

25

Conversion in Boston

The conversion was a major Navy Yard operation and the crew and officers moved ashore and into the tremendous Fargo Building, which had been converted into a receiving station. Only a skeleton crew aboard was necessary and hence, after many months at sea we adjusted ourselves to life on the beach... and it didn't take long! The crew was divided into port and starboard sections. Each section was able to take 21 days leave, one section at a time. While one section was on leave, the other section had the opportunity to explore Boston. The people of Boston were kind enough to give our official homeport a genuine meaning. They were very friendly and treated us with kindness and generosity. I think most of us ended up with a lot of wonderful memories about Boston.

One night I was sitting in the USO talking with some sailors when two pretty girls walked in and asked the director if they could have about a dozen sailors to take along with them to a party. They announced over the PA system that any sailor interested in going to a Halloween party should report to the desk. It didn't take long before the girls had their 12 sailors and I was one of them. We all walked down to the subway station and the girls paid the fares for all of us. We soon were on our way to the suburbs and after about a 15 minute ride we arrived at our destination which I think was Somerville. After a short walk from the station we arrived at what seemed like a real big garage, decorated for Halloween, bustling with girls and a few chaperons. There were all kinds of things to eat and games, like ducking for apples. Everyone had a great time.

Living in the Fargo Building was a welcome change after being at sea for months at a time. It was like living in a large modest hotel set up dormitory style with rows and rows of beds. I believe we were on the 6th floor.

We had some free time and Jerry Fink and I and a couple of other fellows made dungaree liberty over at the Greasy Spoon. It was a diner across the street from the Fargo Building where we went for coffee and to talk to the waitresses. Sometimes we went for breakfast rather than eating Navy chow. By the latter part of December, we departed and proceeded to Norfolk, and then on to training in the

Chesapeake Bay. By this time many of us had been together on many a Christmas Day at various places and we were not surprised to find ourselves anchored in the heart of the bay when the occasion arrived. Only one of our shipmates was lucky enough to spend Christmas off of the ship.

Our Captain received a letter from the mother of a shipmate's girlfriend. It stated that her daughter was in a family way, a certain sailor was responsible, and she thought he should do something about it. The Captain spoke to him about it, asked him if he was responsible, and what he wanted to do about it. He offered to get him a good lawyer if he wanted to fight it or to give him leave if he wanted to get married. The sailor went off to get married while all of the rest of us sat in the middle of the Chesapeake Bay. I often wondered if his decision to do the right thing was influenced by the opportunity to get leave over the holiday.

Upon the completion of our training, we proceeded to New York, where we stayed for less than two days. Those who were not on duty will never forget the New Year's celebration prior to our embarkation for the Pacific. I will also remember that last night in New York City because I was one of those unfortunate ones who had to stay aboard for duty.

26

The Pacific

On New Year's Day we left 36th Street Pier, New York City at about 1600 en route to the Panama Canal Zone. This trip promised warmer days and smoother sailing as we escorted a British carrier also headed for duty in the Pacific.

We arrived at the Panama Canal Zone on January 8 and started to go through the Canal about 1500. We passed through the other end at about 2100 and tied up in Balboa an hour later. On January 9 we left Balboa at 1500 en route to San Diego, California. We arrived there on January 17 and by January 20 we were en route to Pearl Harbor escorting a troop ship, APA 166. We finally arrived in Pearl Harbor on January 26, at 1100.

It wasn't until then we found out about the type of duty we might expect. Because our ship had been converted to an Auxiliary Personnel Destroyer, we possessed most of the advantages of a Destroyer Escort as well as additional ones. We had more fire power, enlarged living quarters to accommodate extra men and officers, four landing boats, a large cargo hatch with cargo handling booms and a grotesque paint job which easily blended in with the palms and foliage of the tropics. We were also attached to the Amphibious Forces. It didn't take much imagination to figure out what kind of work we would be doing, and yet no one ever imagined we would end up doing the work we did. Before long we became familiar with Underwater Demolition Team (UDT).

At Pearl Harbor we were told we would soon be in a fighting Navy. The campaign at Iwo Jima was in its climactic stages and the gigantic offensive in the Philippines was well underway. Meanwhile, we made good use of our time in Honolulu and on the beaches of Waikiki, and Jerry Fink and I decided to get tattoos. I think we had quite a few drinks, though, before we found a tattoo shop. We went in and watched them do their work for quite some time, then decided to go for it.

I got one on my left upper arm designed with an anchor, eagle and the American flag. Jerry decided on a tattoo of his wife's name, Dorrie, on his shoulder. It was interesting to watch the lady do our tattoos. She used something like an electric pencil with two or three needles pulsating in and out. She first took the picture of the tattoo, like a stencil, and transferred it to our arms and then traced over it with an electric pencil. When she filled in the different colors, it hurt some but not too bad. The next morning we found out a few other fellows got tattoos as well. We had to be careful to keep it clean and not get sunburned or it could really get sore. Some of the Officers and old salts tried to scare us with stories about how they could get sore and infected and if we couldn't work we wouldn't get paid. Luckily, we managed to survive without any problems.

On January 29, we got underway and proceeded to Maui for a few days of scheduled exercises. By February 5, we were on our way back to Pearl Harbor loaded with supplies and spent February 10 to the 12th floating in dry dock having our sonar heads inspected and barnacles scraped from the hull of our ship. On the 14th we went back to Maui and the Underwater Demolition Team # 4 arrived on board. They filled our extra living space with 100 men and our cargo hatch with powerful explosives. These men were highly trained demolition specialists and swimmers whose mission roughly was to make reconnaissance of beaches and destroy underwater obstructions in preparation for initial amphibious assaults.

They were the first team the Navy had and in the Philippine invasion they took a direct hit on one of their boats and lost some of their men. Upon their arrival on board, we moved out into the harbor and anchored for a few days where they let the fellows swim off of the fantail. We had to have two boats in the water continuously circling the ship. Each boat was manned with a rifle carrying sailor who watched for sharks. We were anchored off the island of Maui and were told there was a leper colony nearby.

On February 15, we left Pearl Harbor and proceeded west to the Philippines. Our trip included the customary stops at Enewitok, Marshall Islands, and on March 4, we anchored in Leyte Gulf just in time to become the object of an enemy air raid. It was 0400 and a Japanese plane dropped four bombs about 2000 yards from the USS Loy, hitting the beach of Leyte. We continued our training while we were there, joined other ships, and awaited movement orders. We also found a way to work in a few beer parties on the beach. We didn't mind at all.

27

Okinawa

By March 21, we were underway escorting a large task force headed north. We quickly learned the nature of our operation...the invasion of Okinawa. On the March 25 we arrived off the coast of three small islands 30 miles west of Okinawa where mines exploded and "Kamikazes" crisscrossed the sky. At 0620 Japanese suicide planes attacked us. They hit the four following ships: the USS Kimberly (DD 521), USS Gilmer (APD 11), USS Knudson (APD 101) and one unidentified ship. Six Japanese planes splashed down that morning, and one of them fell less than 1500 yards ahead of us. We experienced two more air-raids that night. One was at 1800 and the other was at 2330 when three more Japanese planes were shot down near us.

The main assault was scheduled for April 1 or "Love Day" in the Navy lingo, "Easter Sunday" in the phraseology of our families at home. We arrived early so that the UDT could proceed with its business. We remained late in our alternate capacity as an escort or screening vessel, and we screened an island rather than participated in a convoy against submarines and aircraft.

On the March 27, we approached Okinawa and went within 6,000 yards of the beach to look around. Part of the 5th fleet was bombarding the beach and some of the battleships were as follows: Idaho, Nevada, Tennessee, West Virginia, Arkansas, (where my buddy Tom Parsons was on board), Maryland, and various others. Cruisers of the 5th fleet were: Philadelphia, Portland, Salt Lake City, Wichita, Biloxi, and Cleveland. They bombarded the island all day, shooting over our heads most of the time and withdrew that evening when they steamed in formation about 70 miles north of Okinawa.

On March 28, at 0630, we had another air raid. A Japanese Kamikaze flew over our formation and tried to suicide dive on the USS Kline (APD 120) but overshot his target and crashed just aft of their fantail. Checking the wreckage on their fantail, they were able to prove it was their guns that hit him and were credited with shooting down the plane. The battle fleet bombarded Okinawa all day and we withdrew in the evening. All APDs were assigned to screen the transports (troop ships). We had two more air raids that night.

On March 29, our UDT left the ship and made a reconnaissance of the beach at 1530. I will do a little explaining here to help you envision what happened. The Underwater Demolition Team comparable to the Navy Frogmen of today. They wore a pair of swimming trunks and had a pair of flippers on their feet. Also, they wore a set of goggles, carried a large knife and had no oxygen tank. Before they left the ship they painted their shoulders and face with silver paint so when they surfaced they looked like white caps in the water.

Our team was assigned a certain stretch of the Okinawa beach and the UDT went in to see what obstacles were along the beach that might possibly prevent us from landing with troops. Our ship had to get within a couple miles of the beach to send in our landing boats filled with almost 100 men of the UDT. We did this during the day and the goal was to get as close to shore as possible without being seen so as not to draw gunfire. We dropped the men off into the water and they swam ashore under water. If they came up for air we hoped they looked like white caps in the water.

When they got to the beach, they spread out so they covered a large area, looking for natural hazards, as well as anything like railroad rails, ties, or steel rods that might have been driven into the beach to prevent boats from landing. Each swimmer had a wrist watch and when it was time for the men to swim back to the boat, it was understood that they were to all swim out at exactly the same time for the same distance. When they got back to the ship they all sat down together to painstakingly describe what they saw and mark it down on a map. Sometimes this was done a couple times before they got all the information they needed.

Our boats started at one end of the beach and slowly cruised by towing a rubber boat behind with a man aboard who carried a big steel hook. As the boat passed the swimmers, the man with the hook reached out to the swimmer who grabbed it and was pulled safely back into the boat. If he missed the boat for any reason it was understood he would swim back to the beach and hide from the enemy until they came back, which might not be until the next day. Fortunately, all UDTs arrived back aboard the Loy at 1730 with no casualties. A few had the chills and the doctor had whiskey for medicinal purposes to warm them up pretty fast.

The same night we were assigned a certain sector that kept us far enough away from the transports. They claimed that when the APDs were near them we attracted the Kamikaze. On March 30 at 0730 while approaching Okinawa from our night station, we were directed to go to the assistance of the LSM 188, which sent out a distress signal. A Kamikaze leaving 3 dead and 12 badly wounded and 10 other casualties hit her at 0610. Many of the bodies were mangled and torn beyond recognition.

The Loy came to the rescue giving medical help and much of our damage control equipment. After fighting the fire for some time we were able to save the ship and take the survivors to the Hospital Ship. Later in the morning, after the fleet had been bombarding the island most of the morning, our UDT went in with five or six other teams to blow up their targets. Besides their regular gear they only carried 50 pounds of explosives on their backs. All teams worked together and by noon ten miles of beach were blown sky high. The operation was a success and our team arrived safely back aboard without any casualties. Little did we know we would have another air raid that night!

Once again, on March 31, the fleet bombarded the beach all day long. Many planes from the carrier forces bombed the island and strafed the beaches. We withdrew that night and steamed with the Western Attack Group, 30 miles west of Okinawa.

28

Invasion of Okinawa April 1, Easter Sunday

We returned to Okinawa with the invasion force and were attacked at 0645 by three Japanese planes. Almost every ship present fired on them, including us. The first two planes were shot down immediately. The third plane, a dive bomber, dropped two bombs very close to the cruiser USS Philadelphia and then was shot down. The plane crashed near one of our ship's boats and they salvaged part of the landing gear and brought it aboard.

At 0830, the first wave of troops hit the beach, supported by the naval guns of our battleships and from 300 to 400 carrier planes. There were approximately 1400 ships included in the invasion force. By 1100, two of the airstrips were in the hands of the Americans and our boat crews of Underwater Demolition Team lead the first wave of troops onto the beaches.

At 1900, we had another air raid. One of the planes hit ahead of us and dove into the battleship West Virginia, hitting her on the port side. At 1945 a boat came along side with six marines and a coxswain. Their ship left without them and didn't come back until morning so we fed them and sent them on their way. By 2330, the DE 664 was bombed and at 0230 on Monday April 2, the Skirmish AM 303 reported two mast head bombing attacks and one of her 20mm guns had been knocked out. They had one very serious casualty and requested a doctor. Fortunately, we had one on board.

At 0540 two Japanese planes attacked us and were both shot down and one of them fell just astern of us. By 0700, we anchored in the bay just off of Okinawa. We got underway at 1700 and proceeded to our night station, which was on the outer screen. However, at 1840, five Japanese planes attacked us. We shot down four and the other made a suicide dive, directly hitting the USS Dickerson APD 21. The dive started a huge fire and two explosions. The toll of men lost wasn't set at that time because they were still looking for survivors.

On Tuesday April 3, we went to general quarters at 0130 and no planes came within six miles of us. At 0600, two Japanese planes flew over but no damage was done. That morning we saw the Hospital

Ship, Solace, on the horizon and at 0800 we dropped anchor off the coast of Okinawa. About 1900, we were called to general quarters but no planes ever reached our vicinity. We were shrouded by a thick smoke screen. It covered all ships in the bay.

There were hundreds of ships anchored in the bay of Okinawa and a lot of the ships had smoke generators on their fantails to ensure discretion. When we knew there was going to be an air raid they announced over the TBS voice radio between ships to make smoke. When all ships turned on their smoke generators, the whole anchorage was covered. Although incoming enemy planes could not see us, we couldn't see them either unless we used radar. We avoided doing that because we ran the risk of giving our direction away.

We secured from general quarters at 1930 and everything was quiet until our Underwater Demolition Team touched off 20 tons of TNT at the stroke of midnight! The blast cleared out the reefs along the beaches so our landing craft could land safely.

On April 4, we anchored as before and to our surprise we experienced no air raid that morning. Perhaps this was due to the fact that our "night fighters" planes that fly at night had just arrived. We saw occasional artillery fire on the mountains of Okinawa but remained safe, otherwise. We got underway at 1700 and headed to our night station Able 19 and again there was no air raid. To understand this a little better, picture a big harbor filled with a lot of ships. Stations were set up around the outer perimeter of the harbor about 20 or 30 miles out from the harbor and on a large circumference maybe 10 or 15 miles apart. A ship was assigned to each of these stations day and night (especially at night) to protect the ships in the harbor from submarines, aircraft, or surface ships.

Every once in a while we encountered suicide boats. They were loaded with explosives and tried to run themselves into enemy ships. Even the ships in the harbor had to be careful because if they anchored too close to shore they had to watch for suicide swimmers. The trained combatants tried to attach explosives to the side of the ship or climb up the anchor chain and kill sailors in their sleep. When we were out patrolling on station we didn't make smoke so we were pretty vulnerable out there.

On April 5, we were patrolling station Able 19 and were directed to look for a friendly plane that had crashed in our vicinity. After searching the area for an hour we gave up hope of ever finding the plane or pilot. We kept patrolling the same station all day and night. That day, two years prior, I had been sworn into the Navy.

On April 6, at 0830, we anchored in the bay off the shore of Okinawa. At approximately 1545 we had a surprise air raid. One Japanese suicide plane sneaked in over our ships before anyone knew what was going on. It came in over the transports, right down our port side and crashed in the water 200 yards ahead of our ship. By the time general quarters sounded and before our guns were ever manned, the plane crashed. Twenty minutes later a Japanese plane came in on our port side at a distance of about five miles. He dove but was hit. Not more than three minutes later we sighted another Japanese plane on our starboard bow. It made a long suicide dive for our ship while practically every ship in the bay fired at him without success.

We continued to fire shots from our 5 inch and 40 mm guns. We were pretty sure our last shot from our 5 inch hit the target because just as we fired at the plane it blew up and crashed into the water. Evidently there was some question as to whether or not our gun hit the plane. Some thought we did, others thought we didn't. Personally, I don't know but it certainly looked as if we hit it, making a total of three Japanese planes shot down within the hour.

A few minutes later, two more planes flew over and everyone fired. It was too late by the time the planes were identified as friendly. Both planes were shot down and the pilots killed. They were identified later as one TBF Avenger and one F4F Wildcat. Quite a few fellows felt bad about this terrible mistake. Our ship only fired a few shots because we saw they were friendly soon enough. This started quite an argument.

Many of the fellows claim they shouldn't have flown over the ships because the control was Yellow, which meant we were supposed to fire at every plane in the area. Anytime they reported we might have an air raid, they usually announced flash Red Control Green indicating an air raid is imminent but don't fire unless you are sure it's enemy because friendly planes were also in the same area. Flash Red Control Yellow meant an air raid was imminent and we could fire at anything in the air because there were no friendly planes in the area. So, since it was Control Yellow they should not have been flying over the anchorage.

We got word that there was a great air battle in progress about thirty miles away and some of the ships in the outer screen were reported under attack. As the evening progressed, we continued to get reports of our ships in the outer screen getting hit by bombs and suicide dive bombers. Before long we had a list of 14 ships that were hit. They were as follows: USS Rodman DMS 21, Hyman DD 732,

Wittier DE 636, Howarth DD 592, Beatty DD 528, Panamint AGC 13, Calhoun DD801, Bush DD529, Newcomb DD 586, Devastator AM 318, Morris PG 417, Leary DD 667, Young DD 793, and the Leutze DD 481. The crew of the Beatty later reported they were abandoning ship. I am glad to say the rest of the evening was rather quiet.

At 0330, on April 7, we again received reports Japanese planes were approaching. We immediately made smoke so as to disguise our ships. A few planes flew over and one of them dropped a bomb right near our port side. By 0600 everything was all clear again and we secured from general quarters. However, by 0900 three more ships were reported hit. They were the Bennett DD 473, the Hobbs Victory, and the Wesson DE 184. The Hobbs Victory was an ammunition ship and was blown sky high without any survivors.

That evening we were sent out to the outer screen to station Able 19 and Able 20. At 2100 the ship next to us reported shooting down a Betty. Some of our lookouts reported seeing the plane going down in flames.

On April 8, we had the regular dawn alert at 0530, everything was quiet and we were secured by 0610. I went down below and I wasn't in the sack more than five minutes when the mighty 5 inch went off and the general quarters alarm rang. I dashed up to the bridge in time to see a Japanese plane coming in from dead ahead and low on the water. Our 5 inch main battery was fired and the plane turned and ran. We fired 27 rounds of 5 inch shells at him and it must have been more than he wanted!

There was also a destroyer way out on the horizon that was also firing at him. As the plane got between us and the destroyer, shells started bursting very close to us. The explosions got closer and closer and finally one of them hit the water not more than 300 feet from our starboard beam. We had to reverse our course in order to keep from getting hit. Soon, another destroyer shot down a Japanese plane not more than five miles from us.

29

Yamato

Later in the morning our Captain made a very nice speech, which we were all glad to hear. He announced that the Carrier Task Force 58 had sunk the prize of the Japanese, which was a 45,000 ton battleship, the Yamato. It suffered eight torpedo hits and eight large bomb hits. In addition, there were two cruisers and three destroyers sunk or damaged and three more were left burning although they escaped. The group was attacked southeast of Japan and was heading towards Okinawa. Apparently the Japanese had a big plan to throw everything at us to stop the invasion of Okinawa.

The Carrier Task Force 58 also announced they shot down 1500 Japanese planes in the past seven weeks. On April 6 they shot down 236 planes alone, and 182 Japanese planes got through to Okinawa and attacked American ships. Of those 182 planes, 22 of them made successful suicide attacks and 116 others were shot down by our ships and planes. That was a very good score and it made everyone glad to hear it. The Captain also congratulated all hands on the way we had conducted ourselves during those past harrowing days.

By 1100 we were anchored again off Okinawa. At 1143 the USS Starling AM 64 reported a torpedo had been fired at her while she was patrolling station Able 21 which we passed earlier in the morning. At 1600 we got underway and went out to our night station Able 13. At 1945, the US Gregory DD 802 reported a suicide dive bomber hit her in her forward fire room and that she could still proceed at 15 knots. She shot down two other planes in the same attack.

On April 9, we had the regular sunrise alert but no planes flew within our vicinity. We were again anchored off of the coast of Okinawa by 0930. At 1700 we got underway and proceeded to our night station, Charlie 23, where we also were to be radar guard ship. We manned our guns at sunset but no planes ever came near. It looked as if our night fighters were stopping a lot of the Japanese planes.

However, at 1900, the USS Hopping APD 51 reported she was hit port side by Japanese coastal guns. She took six direct hits from a Japanese six inch gun and her casualties were light considering how hard she was hit. One man from the Underwater Demolition Team was killed and there were quite a few casualties from the UDT and ship's company. The LCS 36 also reported she had been hit by a Japanese suicide plane.

On April 10, at 0800, we proceeded into the anchorage and requested to refuel. By 1000 we refueled alongside the AO Brazos. It was rather rough and we had a hard time but we did it even though they lost three of their fenders.

At 1700 the UDT was transferred to the PA 58 because they did not want to lose any more of their fellows unnecessarily. They claimed they would be in too much danger if they stayed aboard much longer and that they would return in a few days. At 1830 we proceeded out to our night station, Able 29. The weather was bad so it was a quiet night.

On April 11, we were still patrolling Able 29 until about 1030. We were ordered to return to the anchorage to re-embark the UDT. By 1800 they were back aboard and we went out on patrol at station Able 58 for the rest of that quiet night. The next day we anchored in the bay off Okinawa by 0800. At 1300 the USS Waters APD 8 tied up alongside of us to give us 10 tons of explosives. An hour later we went to general quarters because the Japanese tried another desperate large scale suicide dive bombing attack. Our planes stopped most of them before they got within 20 miles of us. In fact, they shot them down like flies. A total of three planes broke through, reached our ships and tried to make suicide attacks but they were shot down before they reached their objectives.

A total of five of our ships were hit in the outer screen and they were as follows: Riddle DE 185, Rall DE 304, Purdy DD 734 possibly, DE 634 and MS 32. On that day alone our planes shot down a total of 111 Japanese planes.

30

Ie Shima

On Friday, April 13, at 0530 in the morning we got underway and headed to the island of Ie Shima. Our UDT went ashore at 0930 with a couple boatloads of explosives. There they contended with a battleship and three cruisers bombarding the island as they went ashore. By 1200, the UDT blew up all of their targets and returned to the ship without one casualty. We expected to be fired upon by coastal artillery and other shore batteries, but to our surprise, nothing happened. By 1230 the operation was over and by 1530 we were again anchored off the coast of Okinawa.

The following morning we got underway at 0600 and went up to Ie Shima. All morning our ships and planes blasted the island with shells and bombs. Our UDT also went in on the beach and blew up a few more objectives. By 1200 we were on our way back to the anchorage and by 1240 we anchored off the coast of Okinawa for the rest of the day.

On April 15, we got underway at 0530 and moved toward Ie Shima for operations. We finished up by 1100 and again anchored off Okinawa by 1200. At 1830 a few Japanese planes came our way and within an hour ten planes flew over; we shot down three of them. The battle caused a few fires on the beach and within minutes the ships were covered by smoke. We received orders not to fire on any plane unless we actually saw it. Throughout the night Japanese planes came over in groups of two or three and occasionally bombed us. On April 16 at about 0300, a Japanese plane dove on our ships and we fired on him. We must have scared him because he leveled off and flew right over our ship at almost masthead height and wasn't seen thereafter. At 0430 we got underway and proceeded to Ie Shima, where we heard that President Roosevelt died in his sleep on April 12, 1945.

31

Invasion

At 0800, the first wave of troops hit the beaches of Ie Shima. Our battlewagons bombarded the island while planes strafed and bombed overhead. At about 0930 a group of Japanese planes came in very low. In fact they were so low we did not detect them until they were almost upon us. The first one tried to hit one of our cruisers but was shot down before it hit its mark. Another plane made a suicide dive for the USS Simms APD 50 but it missed and crashed into the water beside her. The plane came so close to hitting her though that its wing just nipped the mast and ripped off a small piece.

Another plane came in very low and tried to hit the USS Simms, but right before it was about to hit, three Corsairs dove down and shot it out of the sky. Another plane came in on our starboard bow and we fired at it with our 5 inch gun. It was a little out of range although it later crashed into the water from other gunfire. A total of 10 planes were shot down that morning, all within visual range of our ship. At least 85 planes were shot down in the Okinawa area. Five of our ships were hit by suicide planes and one, if not two, were sunk out of the five. Of these five ships three were destroyers, one as a destroyer escort, and an LSM. The rest of the day was very quiet and we anchored at Okinawa at 1900.

On April 17, a plane flew over the anchorage at 0300 but did not drop any bombs. We got underway at 0600 and proceeded to Ie Shima where our UDT blew up a few more targets. By 1700, we were back at Okinawa anchored near Purple Beach. At sunset the gun crews were manned and one Japanese plane flew over without incident.

On April 18, we got underway by 0630 and proceeded to Ie Shima. We anchored 3,000 yards from the beach and three hours later a few shells exploded near our ship. They came from shore batteries so we moved out a little further and dropped the anchor where all was quiet. The UDT continued their operations but had to stop due to too much resistance from the Japanese. There was a lot of sniper fire so they discontinued operations until the army drove the Japanese away from the beaches. We got underway about 1900 and went back to Okinawa to anchor. Two Japanese planes showed up in our area but fortunately didn't stay very long.

On April 19, we got underway at 0530 and proceeded back to Ie Shima. We anchored 2500 yards from the beach and the UDT continued with their operations. We used binoculars and field glasses to actually see our troops fighting on the island. We witnessed our tanks firing and heard the continuous roar of the 155 mm guns coming from Menna Island. We completed our work and went back to Okinawa and were anchored by 1700.

Sadly, Ernie Pyle was reported killed that day along with the troops on the front lines in Ie Shima. He was a famous news correspondent who bravely reported from the front lines right in with the troops. Our ship's boat crew had seen him a few days before.

On the morning of April 20, a Japanese plane flew over and dropped one small bomb off the starboard quarter of the DM 26. She later reported there was no damage done and no casualties. We got underway at 0700 and went to Ie Shima and later returned and set anchor at 1700.

On April 21, we left the anchorage at 0730 and proceeded to Ie Shima for a short while and then went on to the northeastern side of Okinawa where one platoon of the UDT went ashore on a reconnaissance mission. They returned to the ship at 1500 and brought with them a Japanese bicycle. We went back to the anchorage by 1830.

At approximately 1030 the next morning, we raised the American flag over the peak of Ie Shima and on April 22, we went down to Kerama Retto, a small harbor on the southern end of Okinawa. We met the Oiler AO3 and refueled from her.

On April 23, we proceeded back to Ie Shima and dropped anchor near the beach where we gave all our explosives to the Army. We evidently did not need them anymore, and the Army did. We went back to Okinawa and were assigned to screening station, Baker 26. Relieved that the rain kept us safe from attack that night, we patrolled the station for most of the following day and then transferred to Able 37. We patrolled the station until early morning and on April 25, when they announced we were to leave Okinawa. At 0800 we joined the convoy we escorted.

The convoy consisted of approximately 18 LSTs and 24 LSMs, which were landing crafts, used for invasions. The LSTs carried troops and had a flat bottom so that they could go up onto the beach. There they opened the bow and the troops walked directly onto the beach. The flat bottom design also allowed them to carry mechanized equipment such as trucks and tanks.

Our job was to escort the following ships: Three sub chasers, three minesweepers and one patrol craft. The commanding officer of the USS Loy was screen commander and we were underway proceeding on course 156 degrees at a speed of 8 knots. Our destination was Guam by way of Saipan.

On April 26, we continued with a new course of 119 degrees and a speed of 9.5 knots. At 1500 we passed within ten miles of a large convoy going the opposite direction. We guessed they were going to Okinawa. At 1530 we passed within two miles of an aircraft carrier with four destroyer escorts.

On April 27, we steamed on course 121 degrees at 10 knots. On the evening of the 28th, we received a radio report the hospital ship, Comfort, was under air attack and needed immediate assistance. She later reported 47 men were killed by a Kamikaze, but she was proceeding to Guam under her own power.

On April 30, we passed over a volcano where one of the escorts reported a depth of only 8 fathoms of water. On May 1 we arrived in Saipan at 1000 and were released from our duties and told to move on to duties assigned. At 1030 we anchored in the harbor and were underway again by 1800 and proceeded to Guam on course 210 degrees at the speed of 8 knots.

On May 2, we arrived in Guam at 0730 and anchored inside sub nets by 0740. We then set port routine for the first time in at least six weeks and we even had a movie on the fantail. On May 3, we observed normal port routine and took on supplies for most of the day while the Underwater Demolition Team disembarked.

Between May 4 and May 10, we repainted the ship, refueled and took on more supplies. The crew was issued green working uniforms and a pair of working shoes. The Sonarmen had wanted a coffee maker in the Sonar shack for quite some time. If we wanted coffee we had to go below and get it from the galley or mix our own in a pot and take it down to the boiler room where we pushed a steam coil down in the pot to heat it up. We decided it was a good time to make our request. Jerry Fink got permission and a requisition from our division officer and Jerry and I went ashore. We ran our legs off, saw a lot of people and went through a lot of red tape but when we arrived back on the Loy we had a brand new coffee maker. We made a stand to hold it along with all the other things we needed to go with it.

From then on we enjoyed fresh coffee whenever we wanted. Each Sonar watch was responsible to maintain a neat and tidy coffee area and have a fresh pot of coffee ready for the next watch. After we got the coffee maker we usually furnished coffee to anyone on the bridge who wanted it including the officers. For some reason the Captain never drank any. I don't know if he didn't approve of us having it, but he always looked the other way when someone came in for coffee, and he proceeded to get his from the wardroom. It took him weeks to finally ask us for a cup of coffee.

On May 11, we got underway at 1600, heading to Okinawa with the Goldsboro APD 32, the AO 36, and the APA 161. Our base course was 301 degrees and our speed was 15 knots. We arrived in Okinawa at 1200 on May 15 and went to Kerama Retto, arriving at 1600 and where we refueled from the K 115. At 1800 we got underway and made our way to night station, Baker 29. It was then reported an enemy air raid from the west was imminent.

On May 16, at 0230, about 30 enemy planes circled the area. Some flew right overhead but never attacked. Everything was quiet during the rest of the day until 2330; one plane attempted a suicide dive on the USS Ringness APD 100 stationed right next to us. The plane missed the ship, went out and circled and came in again for another dive. He failed and crashed and burned close to the Ringness without causing damage or casualties to the ship. The plane was said to be a Val dive bomber.

On May 17th we were still patrolling Baker 29 and after refueling from the AO 22 we were sent to patrol Baker 26. That evening Kerama Retto and Ie Shima were bombed. At 2130 the DD 779 reported a Japanese plane hit and she had quite a few casualties.

On May 18, we left station Baker 26 at 0630 and moved ahead on course 110 degrees at 17 knots. We were supposed to meet a convoy about 300 miles out and escort them back to Okinawa. At 1800 we met a merchant ship and two escorts. The merchant ship was the Clorvis Victory escorted by the USS Grady DE 445 and also one APD. We believed the Clorvis Victory carried a cargo load of ammunition or something important enough to require four escorts. We arrived back safely at Okinawa at 1000 the next morning and learned the merchant ship was carrying fog oil and spare parts for the smoke screen generators which were badly needed by most ships.

On May 19, we patrolled Baker 31 and all ships were warned to expect a large air raid that night and to also be on the lookout for a new type of robot bomb. Thankfully, no one ever showed up.

On Sunday May 20, we left Okinawa at 0400 with the USS Barr APD 39 and joined another convoy to escort them to Okinawa.

At 1600 we met the convoy which was a group of about 20 ships. We took station #5 and proceeded back toward Okinawa. Among the escorts with us were the USS Bates APD 47 and the USS Chief AM 312. We heard over the aircraft radio they were having quite an air raid back at Okinawa. I guess it was good we weren't there.

We arrived safely with the convoy at 0900 on the eastern side of Okinawa. At 1530, we moved ahead to our night station, Able 34 Able. We were at general quarters most of the evening and at 2100 the USS Bates APD 47 reported she had been attacked. The Bates was in Baker 25 which we patrolled two days prior. She shot down two Japanese planes and it looked as if the "Lucky Loy" left just in time again. A little later the LCS 119 reported she shot down two more enemy planes. Most of these planes had come in low on the water and were not detected by radar until they were almost on top of us.

On May 22, we were still patrolling Able 34 Able. We had general quarters but most of the enemy planes seemed to be heading towards Ie Shima. At 2330, one plane flew right by us at 400 feet and attacked the DMS 29 in station Able 36 Able located just two stations over from us. They splashed one plane and an LCI also reported a submarine fired a torpedo and just missed her bow. Thankfully, the rest of the night was quiet.

On Wednesday May 23, we patrolled Able 34 Able. We left our station long enough to refuel from a tanker at sea, and were back on station by 1600. At 1920, we went to general quarters and stayed in that condition all evening. Many groups of enemy planes came in from the north and northeast. A few of them bombed our ships but most of them bombarded Ie Shima and Yonton airfield on Okinawa. One bomber was seen exploding in midair off our port bow. It was a very large explosion and it was believed the bombs blew up with the plane. There were quite a few planes shot down that night, but I don't believe any ships were hit.

We learned the USS Chase APD 54 was attacked the week before. A Japanese plane attempted a suicide dive but missed and crashed into the water close by. It caused a heavy underwater explosion that ripped open a lot of seams, flooding the engine room crew's quarters. We were relieved when we heard the report of no casualties. The USS Chase was a ship from our old division when the Loy was a destroyer escort.

32

Kamikaze

On Thursday, May 24, 1945, we were still patrolling Able 34 Able. Everything was quiet all morning and the Captain announced we were to celebrate "Holiday Routine." He said he wanted to let the crew get some sleep because there was a chance we might be up all night. At 1730 we went to general quarters and many Japanese planes were reported coming in from the northeast. From radio reports we could hear many of the planes were being shot down by our night fighters. Still, a lot of enemy planes came in and bombed Ie Shima and Okinawa and started a few large fires, which could be seen miles away.

It was a beautiful night for an attack. The sea was calm and the almost full moon lit the clear skies. There were enemy planes reported all around us and one of our night fighters shot down a few Japanese planes. Two radar picket ships reported an encounter with enemy torpedo boats going at speeds from 25 to 40 knots.

Raid after raid of Japanese planes came in throughout the night. Many of the raids had six to ten planes in them, and there were a total of forty raids. One plane was tracked in from sixty miles on our air plot and when it was directly overhead a night fighter shot it down from a very high altitude. The plane burst into flames and came straight down in a ball of fire and crashed into the sea about two miles from us. I will never forget that thunderous sound. The USS Grady DE 445 went over to examine the wreckage and found three Japanese bodies and according to the broken wristwatch worn by one of the pilots, the plane crashed at 12:01.

On Friday, May 25, at twelve minutes after midnight, we picked up three enemy planes on our radar at fifteen miles out. The range closed and we saw the planes were heading directly toward us. As they got within three miles of us they veered off to the right and headed directly for the USS Barry APD 29, which was in Able 33 Able, the next station over from us. The crew of the Barry fired and got some good hits on one of the planes that finally crashed into the starboard side of her, right under the bridge. It was a two engine bomber that hit her, and ripped a big hole in her starboard side causing a large fire in her forward crew's compartment. The crew abandoned ship and the PCE 485 picked up survivors. We also went to her aid and took 15 survivors aboard, two of whom were seriously injured.

We then moved to the north of her to lay a smoke screen to cover the USS Gosselin APD 126 while they attempted to fight the fire on the Barry. While we did this, three more planes attacked ships a few miles away. We had one seriously injured casualty on board. The doctor operated on him because shrapnel had caused large gaping holes in his back.

Finally, we requested to go into How anchorage so we could get the seriously wounded on a hospital ship. We received permission and, by 0315, headed in. We anchored and transferred the casualties to the larger ship by 0600 when reports of the ships hit came in. They were as follows: USS Barry APD 29 hit in station Able 33 Able, USS O' Neill DE 188 hit in station How 158, USS Roper APD 20 hit in our station, Able 34 Able that we had left a few hours before (no wonder we were called the "Lucky Loy"), USS Butler DMS 29, USS Storm DD 780, USS Seilvening DE 441, USS Cole DE 641, USS Spectail AM 305, LCI 135and USS Bates APD 47 hit in station Able 38 Able. She and the DE 441were attacked by seven planes. Five were shot down and the other two hit the Bates.

On May 26, at 1000, we were directed to proceed to Able 34 Able for screening. At 1600 we went to general quarters. The PC 1600 reported she was hit by two Kamikazes and was abandoning ship. There were enemy planes in the area until 2000 even though they didn't hit any more ships.

Sunday, May 27 we continued to patrol Able 34 Able and at 0745 we went to general quarters and eight "Vals" (dive bombers) were reported coming in from the northeast. The USS Forrestal DMS 24 reported she was under attack and wanted a combat air patrol immediately. She later reported she was hit. The DD 630 also reported she was hit and burning fiercely. She said two magazines blew up and there were some survivors in the water who needed immediate assistance. Four ships were sent out to assist her. Later in the morning we secured from general quarters but kept all gun crews on their guns and alert at all times.

We went back to general quarters at 1930 and many planes were reported in the area. Every now and then ships were seen firing at planes. The Japanese planes had all of the advantages over us that night because the moon was full and there was a low overcast of clouds. Our ships were silhouetted in the moonlight and the clouds were so low a plane could slip in without us seeing him. The worst thing was that there was not one friendly fighter plane in the area. They had set "Flash Red, Control Yellow "which meant air raid was imminent and to fire at anything."

At about 2245, a Japanese plane dropped 15 flares near us and a few minutes later he dropped some more. About 2300, the ship next to us fired at a plane and at 2305 two "Bettys" (twin engine bombers) attacked us on our starboard side. It appeared to us that the one came in to attract our attention while the other tried to hit us. Fortunately we saw both of them in time. We fired at both and one exploded off our starboard bow. The other started to smoke and it turned just in time to miss our fantail. We saw a large explosion when it crashed about a mile astern.

Another plane flew directly over the ship next to us then circled and came straight toward us. Every gun on our starboard side started to fire at it. We believed it was a "Val" dive bomber and her motor burst into flames as she headed in our direction. Our guns fired up until the last moment but it finally hit us on the starboard side aft, right under #3 40mm gun turret. The whole ship shuddered from the explosion and we all knew right away we were hit. The plane exploded, throwing gasoline and oil all over the place and drenched some of our gun crews. A large blaze covered most of the fantail but no one panicked and everyone did a wonderful job of getting the fire out in record time.

We flooded the magazines aft to prevent them from blowing up and within a short time we were underway at a very slow speed. When we were hit we lost all water pressure so all we had to put the fire out with was CO2s and handy billies (portable pumps). Shrapnel went through the mast and cut radar cables and some communication lines. The whole starboard bulkhead was riddled with shrapnel holes and one 40 mm and one 20mm out were out of commission. There were three men killed and about ten men wounded. One fellow was blown overboard and was rescued by another ship. However, soon after they told us that, they got hit.

Our aircraft radar was damaged and inoperative and many other things were put out of order. The two starboard boats were smashed and splintered beyond repair. We reported we were hit and then proceeded back to How anchorage. We made about three knots and it seemed as if we were standing still. Then the payoff came! Another plane circled the ship at two miles, and all of a sudden he started for us, coming in on the starboard side. Every gun that could fire did so and he zoomed over just a few feet above the ship. As he passed over the port side he appeared to be burning and after he got out a little distance the Captain announced that the plane was coming back for more. Just then we saw the plane come in but it never got to us. Instead it exploded and crashed astern of us, giving us another plane to our credit and taking about ten more years off our lives!

Are you wondering where was I during all this excitement? Well, my general quarters' station was usually either on the Sonar or on the Radar. Right before we were hit, I was the radar operator. I picked up the plane that hit us on the radar at about eight miles out. I reported it to the bridge and gave ranges and bearings, as it got closer. When I told them the distance was four or five miles, I heard the five-inch guns firing. When I told them three miles, I heard the 40mm guns firing. When I lost contact I heard the 20mm guns firing and then it hit and the whole ship rolled over to the port side and I was thrown on the deck.

Just as I got up off of the deck and realized I was all right, the door from the pilothouse opened and out came the quartermaster, Roy Perron, who was the helmsman during general quarters. He said "I'm bleeding, I'm bleeding," and when we looked at him we realized what happened. Before we were hit he was at the helm drinking a cup of coffee. He placed it next to the rudder indicator in front of him. The pilothouse was always kept dark at night because the ship is blacked out. The rudder indicator had a red light over it so the helmsman could see it. His coffee had a lot of sugar in it and when the ship got hit, he was knocked down on the deck and felt his warm, sticky arm. When he held it up to the red indicator light it looked like blood and he sort of panicked. We often laughed about that later.

When the plane that hit us was approaching, our #3 40mm gun crew was the first to fire and it came straight in following the tracers. It hit and exploded right below that gun. As the plane came toward the ship, one of the 20mm gun crew took out the empty cartridge magazine and stooped over to pick up the full magazine, and his helmet fell off. He didn't stop to put it back on and when the plane hit, shrapnel hit his head and killed him. His name was W.R. Logan. Most everyone called him Red, because of his bright red hair. He died on his 21st birthday. The other two members of that gun crew were also killed. Their names were T.A. Kelly and B.M. Graves.

The 40mm and the 20mm gun were close together and right behind it was a gun directory. It looked something like a set of bicycle handlebars with a sight on it we could look through to see approaching targets. A sailor was strapped into the director and as he moved the director, the 40mm gun also moved toward the target. When we were attacked my friend, Nolan Noble, was strapped in the director. He did an excellent job directing the 40mm gun at the target, but when the plane exploded his body took a lot of shrapnel. He was seriously wounded and later taken off of the ship.

We slowly headed for How anchorage because we were listing at a pretty good angle and the water poured into the crew's compartment. They gradually pumped the water into tanks on the opposite side of ship and returned the ship to an upright position. We were under the protection of a smoke screen and it seemed like forever getting into the anchorage. The ship's doctor did an outstanding job of operating on some of the seriously injured.

We finally reached the anchorage by 0430 and all hands were mustered to see if anyone was missing. They passed around a ration of whiskey or brandy to warm us up and steady our nerves and don't worry, we all needed it! Before, it seemed like one big show where we watched someone else get hit. But now if someone slammed a hatch, a lot of fellows hit the deck to hide or try to protect themselves.

We tried to get some sleep but at 0530 we were called to general quarters again and another plane attacked us. We shot it down within one thousand feet of the ship, giving us our fifth plane shot down in that one hectic night. We tried to get a little more sleep, but by 0830 we had general quarters again and Zeke attacked us. We shot it down and it crashed right near our fantail, giving us six planes to our credit, and a day we will never forget.

That morning they took the wounded off of the ship and held memorial services for the three dead men. As far as we knew there were at least 10 ships hit that night. Some of them were as follows:

USS Loy APD 56, APD 126, APD 102, DD 630, DMS 629 and APD 81.

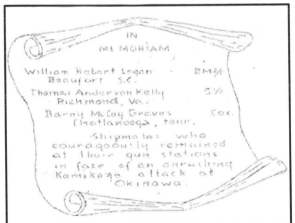

On Tuesday, May 29, we got underway and proceeded to another berth where we tied up alongside the repair ship ARS 28. For the next two days she did some temporary work on the side of our ship. A few days later, we changed berths and tied up alongside the repair ship ARL 8 where they temporarily patched our side so that we could go to the rear area.

On Sunday, June 3, I took communion at the church service on the repair ship ARL 8. We were warned about Japanese suicide swimmers who swam out from the island, slipped aboard undetected and killed as many men as possible. That very thing happened a few nights earlier on the repair ship ARL 8. A Japanese swimmer killed three men before they caught him.

On June 6, we refueled and on June 7 we got underway at 0930 to pick up a convoy. By noon, we set out toward Saipan with the APD 126, the USS O'Neill DE 188 and two other escorts. We accompanied 30 LSTs and APAs. We arrived in Saipan at 1200 on Wednesday, June 13 and anchored in the harbor by 1530. The following day, we loaded 241 bags of U.S. Mail into our cargo hold. After refueling Friday morning, we got underway at 1800 for Leyte in the Philippine Islands. Tuesday afternoon we arrived in Leyte Gulf and were anchored by 1300.

The next morning we tied up starboard side to the destroyer tender Yosemite AD 19 for battle damage repairs. By July 20, 1945, the crew of the Yosemite mended our broken ship. We didn't mind waiting because it gave us a chance to get a lot of rest while we enjoyed some beer parties on the beach. At 0800, on July 20, we left the USS Yosemite AD 19 and refueled from the tanker AOG 41. Unfortunately, we had to discharge 50,000 gallons of fuel the next day

Hauck, Manor, Fidler

94

and prepare to go into dry dock due to an oil leak in the starboard side. By July 23, they were finished and at 0700 we went back to the tanker to refuel. We then made a degaussing run and calibrated the compass.

On July 30, we got underway for the island of Luzon. We arrived the next day and anchored at Legaspi near the Mayon volcano. On August 5, we got underway for maneuvers with the APDs 38, 59, 60, 62, 63, 65, 77 and 123. The next day we practiced having a small invasion. On August 7, we went back to Legaspi and left for Leyte with APD 38 and 65. We anchored in Berth 38 on August 9 and the next day we were informed that the United States dropped an atom bomb on Hiroshima and Nagasaki. On August 15, Japan announced their acceptance of our peace terms. We were very happy because we had been told we were being trained for the invasion of Japan.

Things stood still for a while and we took it easy. Since the war was over, we no longer had to darken the ship and they showed movies on the fantail every night. Boy, it was a nice feeling not to have to worry about the next air raid!

On the evening of September 2, we were watching a movie when all of a sudden a voice over the loudspeaker announced the war was officially over and Japan had signed our peace terms. Just that quick every ship in the harbor blew their whistles, rang their bells and fired their ready pistols which made it seem like the 4th of July. What an amazing sight and feeling that was!!!

VICTORY CELEBRATION

We left Leyte on September 11, 1945, which was the second anniversary of the commissioning of the USS Loy. Upon our departure, we escorted a small aircraft carrier headed for Manila. We passed several small islands when all of a sudden our compasses went haywire. The officer of the deck reported it and the Captain said it was most likely due to a magnetic attraction on the island and that our officers should keep our ship directly in front of the carrier. We did as we were told and at 0800 the next morning we received a message from the carrier, "Congratulations on excellent navigation. Our compass has been out all night and we have been following right behind you." How is that for the blind leading the blind! I am happy to say we arrived safely in Manila and left the next day for Lingayen Gulf.

On September 20, we got underway at 0615 with 23 troop transports, two Patrol Craft and one other APD. We headed for Kobe, Japan and on the night of September 22nd we passed within 100 miles of Okinawa. We received a report that a mine in the area hit a ship, so we were all on edge. We saw many floating mines cut loose by minesweepers. We also encountered live mines and blew up or sank most of them during the day. When it got dark it was another story! The Commodore of the convoy instructed all of the troop ships to line up in one long column and told our Captain to put our ship at the head of the column, and if we couldn't sink or blow up the mines we better hit them with our ship before they hit us! Boy, and I thought the war was over!

We managed to get through the next couple days and destroyed a lot of mines, during the day and some at night. Since the water was calm we picked up some mines on radar and shot at them when they were close enough to see. To play it safe though, the Captain made everyone who wasn't needed below decks sleep up on the main deck with life jackets on. That way if we hit a mine there would not be as many casualties.

At midnight, on September 25, we arrived at the swept channel and proceeded through it. We sighted a few mines on the way in but all the ships passed clear. We showed up at Wakayama by 0530 and spent the next month there while troop ships unloaded. We weren't allowed to go ashore because we were told it was unsafe. However, some of us went ashore a few times on business.

We experienced an oncoming typhoon during our stay at Wakayama and we rode it at anchor with our engines running full speed into the wind that ran upwards of 130 miles an hour. We survived the storm, refueled on October 25 and left the next day at 1240.

Along with the USS Barber, USS Bassett and the USS Register we proceeded to Nagoya, Japan and encountered another typhoon! The winds were fierce and hit us on the beam. Normally in a storm like that we headed straight into the wind to keep from rolling so much, but since we were still in the channel we had to follow it even though there were mine fields on both sides. At one point we made rolls up to 65 degrees and almost toppled. At the last minute a big wave hit us and got us started back the other way.

Somehow we managed to get out of the channel and headed into the wind. By October 27 we anchored safely in Nagoya, Japan and stayed there until November 1. From there we made our way to Taku, China with a large communications ship by the name of USS Wasatch AGC 9. We arrived early in the morning on November 5 and that same day I went on liberty into the city of Teintsin. We didn't have much time to explore but I came back with a bunch of coins with holes in the middle.

When I got back to the ship I found out that I had enough points to get discharged. I forget how many points I needed but I was one of the first groups to go home because I had my mother as a dependent. That placed me in the same class as a married man. As you can imagine I was quite surprised to go home after all that time away.

On November 6, I said goodbye to everyone and transferred to the USS Wasatch and the next day we got underway for home. There were 21 of us fellows who left the Loy along with a lot of others from various ships. We were rather crowded but no one seemed to mind! We sat and did a lot of reading, and played a lot of Pinochle, and before we knew it we were in Pearl Harbor.

We arrived on the morning of November 21 and they sent a working party ashore to get a load of turkeys and other things for Thanksgiving. Jerry Fink and I were two of the fellows picked for the job. We were instructed to go to the motor pool, get a truck and driver and make sure that we were back to the ship by 1700 because we had to get out of the harbor before the nets were set.

Well, we got the truck and the driver and filled the truck with turkeys and supplies. As we headed back to the ship our driver stopped at the motor pool and we sat there for a long time until we decided to inquire about what was going on. We found out that our driver went home because his day was finished. So one of our fellows decided to drive the truck back to the ship and we arrived just as they were pulling up the gangplank. They told us to get on the ship and leave the loaded truck because there wasn't time to unload it. Fortunately, the Wasatch still had plenty of food to have a Thanksgiving dinner. The next day we enjoyed a delicious turkey feast!

A few days later, we arrived in San Diego, CA where Jerry Fink and I boarded a troop train headed for Bainbridge, MD. It took us 5 days to cross the country and we were discharged on December 7, 1945. I was in the Navy a total of 2 years, 8 months and 3 days.

Ken Fidler Sonarman Third Class
Sam Metz Sonarman Third Class
John Lund Electrician Third Class
Carl J Fink Sonarman Second Class

Part III

33

Back Home or Getting Settled

I was discharged at the Bainbridge, Maryland naval base where we were given a complete physical before they let us go. I guess that was for their protection so that we couldn't come back and say that we had some disease or something. They tried to draw my blood from about six different places in my arms but never could find a vein. The doctor said I have small veins and it makes it difficult to find them. He finally had to give up after squeezing my arm so much the veins collapsed! He said that since I was going home he guessed it didn't matter if they didn't check my blood. I was relieved to get out of there and head home.

The Navy paid my train fare from Bainbridge to Reading. Home was still 632 Schuylkill Avenue where my mother had been living since I went into the Navy. It was a first floor apartment consisting of a big living room, a small bath, one bedroom, and a big kitchen with a pantry behind it. We also had use of the basement. It was nice to be home again after 32 months in the Navy. Raymond was still in the Army and hadn't returned yet. I think my mother was glad to see me after living there all that time alone.

It didn't take long to get used to being home though and I soon started to look around for a job. In fact, as veterans we were allowed to sign up for unemployment at $50 a week for 52 weeks. I think they used to call it the 50-50 Club. I didn't collect a penny of it because I never even signed up. My one childhood buddy who got out of the Navy about when I did signed up for the club right away. He told them he was a poet when he signed up and they never were able to find him a job. He collected for the whole 52 weeks. Meanwhile, I was fortunate to find a job right away and I started work on January 6, 1946.

34

Back to Work and Getting Started

When I was in high school, I took a technical course and wanted to learn to be a machinist. So as soon as I got out of the Navy I went to the Textile Machine Works to see if I could get a job and found out they had an apprentice program and that they were hiring. I signed up and was able to start right away. Being a veteran, the government paid for my training and bought some of the tools I needed to get started.

The training consisted of a rotation program of working one month and then going to school one month. I had to do this for two years and then the last two years I worked full time. When school was over, I had to decide what direction I wanted to go. In other words, I had a choice of becoming a machinist working in production or I could go on to learn to be a toolmaker, inspector, pattern maker or a machine erector.

I earned 42.5 cents per hour and usually worked 50 hours a week, 10 hours a day and 5 days a week. When I made my monthly returns to the shop, I was placed in different departments so that I would get a wide range of experiences. There were many departments and some of them included drill press, milling, planing, boring, shaping, inspection and assembly. Almost all of the departments were very dirty to work in because we worked with cast iron. The dust from this material turned our hands and clothing black.

I spent the school months at Wyomissing Polytechnic Institute, which was a trade school owned by Wyomissing Industries. The school was about one block from Textile Machine Works and right across the street from Berkshire Knitting Mills. It was on the corner of 8th Avenue and Hill Avenue.

Textile Machine Works was a very big machine shop that built full fashioned knitting machines. These machines knitted 30 full fashioned nylon stockings at one time. These were stockings that had a knitted seam up the back of the leg and fit the leg very nicely.

Berkshire Knitting Mills was a large mill that had many full fashioned knitting machines to make full fashioned stockings.

Narrow Fabric Company had braiding machines that made such things as parachute chord.

Wyomissing Industries owned these three companies. Textile Machine Works built the machines for these two companies.

The government gave me a monthly allowance during the time I was going to school and also paid for my books. For two years we studied Algebra, Trigonometry, Calculus, Chemistry and Chemistry Lab, Physics and Physics Lab, Business Corporation, Materials of Industry, Strength of Materials, Electrical Engineering, Mechanical Drawing, Mechanics in Industry and a few others. I didn't have any form of transportation when I first started so, most of the time, I walked or took a bus or trolley car to and from class and work. At one time the bus and trolley fare was seven cents to your destination, even if you had to transfer to another bus or trolley car. Other times I was able to ride home with one of several friends who lived nearby.

One thing that interfered with my studies a little bit in the beginning was that I had a girlfriend. You may remember I mentioned in Memoirs Part Two about going on a blind date with Bill Morris and two girls. Emily Schultz was my date and she wrote to me pretty faithfully while I was in the Pacific.

When I came home I went to see her in College Point, Long Island. She had an older sister and a younger brother and her parents were very nice. It didn't take long until I started visiting her regularly on the weekends. I left Reading on Friday evenings and came back home on Sunday nights. I had to take the train from Reading to Philadelphia, from Philadelphia to New York, and from New York I took the Long Island train out to College Point. I don't think my mother was too happy with that but she never complained. It not only got a little expensive, but it was pretty hard with all my studies. It didn't last for very long and we finally decided to go our own ways.

35

Ray Arrives Home

Soon after I started to work, my brother Raymond arrived home from the Army and was discharged. He had been in England and he came home on the Aircraft Carrier Lake Champlain. Soon after his return we started to think about moving.

We needed more room and the landlord tried to evict our mother while we were in the service. He bought the house while we were in the service and planned to use the first floor for his electrical business. When he tried to evict our mother he found out that he couldn't do that while her sons were in the service. His name was Schaeffer over around 2nd and Oley Street.

36

Moving or Moving In

Finally we found a house at 839 Pear Street. We decided to go in it together and bought it for around $3,000 on April 24, 1946. At that same time, Ray decided to go to Albright College and we all settled into our new home. It was just what we wanted at the time because it gave us a lot more room and it was in a nice neighborhood. We also had great neighbors. Our facing neighbors were people by the name of Schwartz. He was a bob tailor and had a bakery route. They had two adopted children and lived in a downstairs apartment and rented out the 2nd and 3rd floors for extra income. Our back neighbors were people by the name of Bierman. They had a son, Ralph, who was in my class in high school. While he was in the Navy, he met a girl from Okinawa and eventually married her.

Directly across the street lived a family by the name of Zimmer. They had three sons and two daughters. Their oldest son was Charles; we called him Red because of his red hair. He also worked at Textile Machine Works and went to the trade school just as I did, so, many a time I was able to ride back and forth with him because he owned a car.

Two doors up the street from Zimmer's was a neighborhood grocery store. It was owned and operated by a father and son by the name of Irvin. It sure made it nice to have a store that handy; when we ran short of something we could just run across the street. It was almost like when I was a little boy and we lived next door to a grocery store.

My Aunt Minerva and Uncle Calvin Fidler, who were the parents of my cousin John Fidler, lived at 835 Pear Street when they were first married somewhere around 1912. That was only two houses away from 839 Pear Street. Also John's wife, Mary Frye, told me that either when she was a little girl, or when she was born, they lived at 839 Pear Street or next door at Schwartz's, I'm not sure which it was.

When we bought the house on Pear Street it was in pretty good shape. Ray and I did a few improvements during the next year or so. We decided to either paint or paper the front bedroom on the second floor. We brought the garden hose up through the front window to wet down the wallpaper. We found that there were quite a few layers of paper on the wall and I told Ray that if we got down to a nice paper we liked, we'd quit right there!

Another time we painted the outside of the windows upstairs and Ray used a blow torch to burn the paint off of the wood and something got too hot inside the wall and caught fire. I believe we had the fire department out to our house. I also remember one time I refinished the front door. It was made of oak and looked pretty good by the time I was finished with it.

We had some squirrels that seemed pretty friendly. They came up on the front porch and begged for something to eat and we fed them. One day Ray coaxed a squirrel into the vestibule, quickly closed the door and tried to pick it up. The squirrel was not happy and bit him. Fortunately, he opened the door right away and let it go or he might have been eaten alive.

37

Friends

During my time at Textile, I made a lot of friends. I ran around with Ralph Hill who was from Oley. I also ran around with Felix Ciabatoni. He lived in the 500 block on Schuylkill Avenue which was only a block from where I lived. There was also Henry Simborski and Leonard Bush who lived on Penn Avenue in West Reading. The five of us ran around together when we had a little time. Sometimes on Saturday nights we made the rounds of some of the clubs in Reading. Since Henry was Polish he was able to get us in the Polish American club and the Knights of Columbus. Felix was Italian and got us in the Italian American club. Ralph and Felix had cars and we had a lot of great times together.

38

Wyomissing Polytechnic Institute

The five of us were all in the same class in the Wyomissing Polytechnic Institute, WPI. When we first started, our class consisted of about 23 students. Most of us were veterans except for a few. One of those was an elderly gentleman who seemed to be going back to school because he had nothing else to do. The other fellows had been on the farm during the war. By the time graduation came around there were only six of us left including Ralph, Henry, Felix, Leonard and I. The rest either quit or were let go because they didn't make the grade. We had a lot of rough times because some of the classes were very difficult and I'm afraid most of us just coming out of the service still weren't ready to settle down and take it seriously. Most of us didn't spend enough time studying so we struggled our way through chemistry and calculus! Our chemistry teacher, Mr. Long, was very strict. If the bell rang and you weren't in the room, forget it! He slammed the door shut and you didn't get in for that class.

Some of the students pulled some pretty good, or maybe bad, jokes on some of their classmates. One day we were down in the basement, which was set up with our lockers and a lounge area where we studied and ate lunch. That particular day some of the older fellows decided to pull a joke on one of the younger unpopular fellows. They took two of the tables and put one on top of the other and then they put this fellow in a GI can (big trash can) and then sat the can on top of the two tables. When this was done, the top of the can was only inches from the ceiling and the fellow had no way of getting out. Then everyone went home and left him there. I don't remember quite how it ended up. I think a night watchman found him later and got him down.

We also had an English teacher who was quite a character. His name was Kilbacki and he later became mayor of Reading. He was quite an agitator and somehow managed to get all of us veterans to go out on strike. We marched downtown to some government office. I don't remember what it was all about but the school gave in to us and we then had a party at Egleman's Park. Someone brought beer along even though it wasn't allowed. Mr. Kilbacki had us put the beer right outside of the park where we could get it when we wanted it! He also had an interesting story about how he assigned grades. He said he took everyone's name, wrote it on a slip of paper, placed them in a hat and then threw them up the steps. The one that went on the highest step got the highest grade. Sometimes I actually believed that was the way he did grade us!

39

The Shop

After a month in school it was always pretty nice to go back to work at the shop for four weeks. We learned a variety of skills in each department we rotated to. In the drill press department we didn't just drill holes all day. We also were taught how to sharpen all of the drills and were taught how to set up the jobs. This was the same in most of the departments.

Back in those days, Textile Machine Works didn't pay by check. Instead, every Friday they came around pushing a big cart filled with everyone's pay envelopes with the correct amount of cash in each. I understand that not too long before I started there they used to pay in silver dollars.

As I said before, while we were in the shop we usually worked 10 hours a day and five days a week. We also had to come in on Saturday mornings for five hours for training classes ran by Mr. Schwartz. He was in charge of the apprenticeship program and taught us how to use hand tools as well as how to use a file and scraping tools. Spot filing and scraping were two very important things to learn before you became a machinist. If you chose to be a machine erector you did a lot of spot filing and scraping.

When we started the Saturday morning classes, Mr. Schwartz gave each of us a three inch square cast iron block. The surfaces were rough and not perfectly square with each other. He taught us how to file all the surfaces so that they were reasonably smooth and had each side perfectly square with the other. Once we reached that point, he taught us how to scrape the block on all six sides. Filing and scraping is an art and you don't learn it overnight. It took us quite a while to get the blocks finished to his satisfaction!

The machinist apprenticeship program consisted of 8,000 hours of schooling and shop work combined. This was usually covered in four years, but since we were working a lot of overtime we were able to finish our apprenticeship in less than a four-year period.

40

Transportation

As I said before, Ralph Hill and I ran around a lot and he had a car. I think it was a 1937 Chevrolet and about this time I started to get the itch to get a car for myself. But I first had to get a driver's license. Ralph said if I got a learner's permit he would teach me how to drive and I could practice driving with his car. So, I got the permit and we drove all around the countryside. I didn't seem to have any trouble with that and everything went pretty good. One night I did have a little scare, though. It was a foggy night in Ephrata and I had to get onto a four lane highway. I couldn't see very well and I went up a down ramp and started down the four lane highway in a lane going the wrong direction! Fortunately, there wasn't any traffic and we soon realized my mistake and corrected it in a hurry.

I was happy when Ralph said I could take the driver's test in his car. We drove to Wyomissing and Ralph said he would park it in front of the place as soon as there was room. In the meantime, I went inside and took the written part of the test and my eye test. When I finished, the state policeman told me to go out and get in my car and he would be right out. I started out to the car and I saw that Ralph had parked his car right out in front of the building and behind another car.

I got in the driver's side of Ralph's car and put the clutch in to start the engine. What I didn't realize was that when Ralph parked the car he parked it in reverse and didn't put the brake on. The engine started, but since the clutch was in and the brake was off, the car slowly drifted forward without me realizing it was moving. Just as the state policeman reached the car, I drifted into the car in front of me. What a way to start! I explained to him why it happened and fortunately the rest of my driving must have been satisfactory because he passed me and I got my license.

Whoopee!

So I had a license but no car. However, I was saving my money and got lots of practice driving with Ralph. Now and then I visited my Navy buddy, Bill Morris. He and his wife Marge lived in Hilldale, which was a development right outside of Pottstown. I usually went back and forth on the train and Bill picked me up at the station. Once in a while I hitchhiked.

One time that I visited Bill, one of our Navy buddies also was visiting Bill. We decided to go on a picnic at Montgomery Park. Here is a picture we had taken while we were there.

On one of my visits, Bill excitedly introduced me to his brand new 1947 Chevrolet. He and Marge were planning to go to New York to visit her family on Long Island and they asked me if I would like to go with them. I said, "Sure," and soon after that we went to New York for a weekend. On the way over Bill asked if I would like to drive for the experience and also because it was a new car. I said I would like to drive and he let me drive it about half way to New York.

Around this time in my life, I was also active in the young people's group at St. Matthew's church. I was the president of the group and Lydia and Bob Yeich were the adult sponsors or chaperons. One time our group was invited to some dinner or function up at Bynden Woods up in the mountains behind Wernersville. The group consisted of about ten or twelve boys and girls and we only had Bobby Yeich's car. Finally one of the girls said her father would let her have the car if we had someone to drive it. Well, Bob asked me if I would drive and I reluctantly said yes. I had a car full of mostly girls and I was driving in the mountains where I hadn't been before and it was in the dark. I took it easy, though, and everything went fine and we had a good time.

41

Machine Erecting

They say time goes fast when you are having fun. I guess that is what happened because all of a sudden my first two years of my apprenticeship were almost finished and I had to decide what direction I wanted to go from there. Textile Machine Works was booming, and they were selling so many full fashioned knitting machines that they needed many more machine erectors. The job appealed to me because I might get a chance to travel all around the country and maybe even out of the country. The job also paid better than the shop. Years later I realized this was the best job I ever had as far as enjoying what I was doing and being satisfied goes.

At the end of my two-year apprenticeship, I decided to become a machine erector and was transferred to the erecting floor located in a long very big building. They had a system where a team of frame erectors started at one end of the building and started building the knitting machines from the ground up. They only put up the basic structure, maybe about one third of the machine, which was the bottom third. The machines were 52 feet long, contained a quarter of a million parts, and weighed about 16 tons.

They started out by putting down an oil drip pan that the whole machine rested on and then built the machine on this pan. A group of frame erectors put up the mainframe work with some of the shafting, plus the main drive shaft and everything that goes along with the gear chain. That gave the machine enough weight so they could get it reasonably lined up and leveled. Then they hooked up the motor and ran in the drive shaft a little while. That was about as far as they went before they started on the next machine. The frame erectors continued to build machine after machine, until they got to the end of the building and then they went back to the other end of the building to start all over again.

After the drive shaft of each machine was run in a little bit, a new team of finishing erectors was assigned to it. That is where I started my training to be an erector. Each machine usually had two finishing erectors and one apprentice assigned to it. I was assigned to two old German men who really knew their jobs, but they were hesitant to teach me because they felt threatened by the idea of me knowing too much. Eventually, they came around. We got along well and I learned a lot from them.

They taught me everything that had to be done on these machines before they turned me loose. We divided the length of the machine up into thirds and I worked on my third. That way I really learned everything and it never got boring because each day I was doing something different. There was so much to do, many things to put on the machine, and everything had to be set with gages. We had to constantly plumb the machine straight and repeatedly level the machine, so that it was perfectly straight and perfectly level. If it wasn't straight and level it wouldn't run well and it wore out more quickly.

The three of us built the machine until it was about eighty per cent completed. Then we ran the machine, oiled the bearings and checked that everything was all right and nothing was getting hot. Although we could run the machine, there was a lot more to be done before it could knit stockings. Our part of the process took about 10 to 12 weeks, so you can imagine how much work was needed to build one machine.

After we left the machine another team of erectors came along and got it ready for shipment to the customer. Some of the machines were sent to the customer all in one piece, but this was difficult and they didn't do it too often. They needed special equipment, a special big flatbed truck to carry it, and special permits to take it over certain roads. This was pretty costly and dangerous. Instead, most of the machines were torn down and shipped out in boxes. Certain parts of the machine were torn down as a unit and were packed in big wooden crates and sent out to the customers. An outside erector was assigned to each machine, and he placed oil pans on the floor and rebuilt it all over again. He was responsible for the whole machine and wasn't finished until he had it knit thirty good stockings. Then the customer signed an acceptance paper and at that point the erector got paid a bonus.

The Reading full fashioned knitting machines, at that time, sold to the customer for about $32,000. They claimed that the machine would pay for itself after they ran it around the clock for one year! No wonder the customers were anxious to get them. Each machine made 30 full fashioned nylon stockings at one time, which took about twenty minutes. They were knitted flat and were later seamed up the back, dyed and shaped before they were ready for the marketplace.+

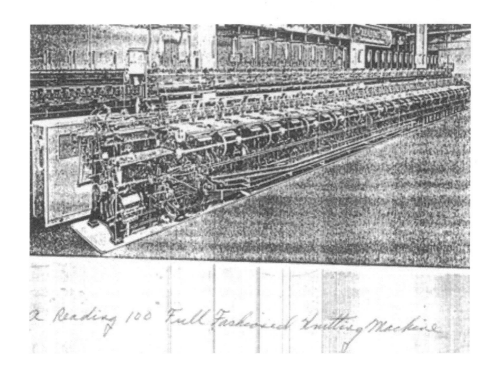

A Reading 100" Full Fashioned Knitting Machine

42

Ray's Graduation

It was the beginning of 1948 by the time I started working on the erecting floor. Ray was a student at Albright College and graduated in May of that year. I still remember the graduation; something happened to make it memorable. I attended the ceremony even though my mother couldn't. She didn't go out of the house very much because she had an ulcerated leg, which gave her a lot of trouble. The graduation was going to be broadcast on the radio and she said that she would listen to it.

The ceremony was held outside on the lawn filled with bleacher type stands. I believe they were all full. I don't remember at what point in the program this happened, but all of a sudden one of the bleachers collapsed. It was loaded with people, and it happened so quickly. People started screaming and our mother heard all of this on the radio and was beginning to wonder what in the world was going on. Then she heard the ambulances and that really worried her. Quite a few ambulances showed up and as far as I remember there were quite a few injuries. I don't remember whether we were able to call and let our mother know what happened or if we had to wait until we got home. What an experience that was!

43

Trolley Cars

In 1948 we still had trolley cars and there are two trolley stories I must tell. The one I was involved in and the other I wasn't. On a Saturday afternoon I was home working around the house and all of a sudden I heard the sound of ambulances. At the time, I wondered what was going on and later on found out. There was a Schuylkill Avenue trolley loaded with high school children on their way to a football game with people standing in the aisles and on the back platform. As they were coming up the hill some of the students were carrying on and one of them pulled on the trolley cable and the trolley came off the wire. This caused the motorman to lose all power and the trolley stopped going forward and drifted backwards down the hill. At the bottom of the hill at Schuylkill Avenue and Windsor Street, there is a sharp curve and the trolley jumped the track. Fortunately, I don't think anyone was seriously hurt!

The next story happened to my mother and I while we were on our way to see Dr. Rothermel about her ulcerated leg. He was our family doctor and he had his office on North 10th Street. We had to take two trolley cars each direction to and from his office. To get home we took the Schuylkill Avenue trolley to Fourth & Penn St. At that point we transferred to the 4th Street Loop trolley that took us to Front & Windsor Streets. The Shillington trolley also went out on 4th Street for one block and it turned right on to Washington Street one way against traffic. When the Shillington trolley went out 4th Street an electric switch automatically changed the track so that they could slowly turn the corner against traffic. After they were around the corner the trolley stopped and the conductor got out with a steel bar that he stuck in the track and changed the track back to the way it was before so that the 4th Street Loop trolley could go straight out 4th Street.

Well, evidently the last Shillington Trolley that went through ahead of us didn't stop to change the tracks back to where they should be. So as we headed over 4th Street and approached Washington Street the traffic light began to turn red. Rather than stopping, the motorman decided to speed up to go through the light. What a surprise he and everyone else had, when instead of flying straight through the intersection and out 4th Street, we went around the corner on two wheels and up Washington Street rocking back and forth!!!

The trolley jumped off the wire and the lights went out and we stopped. Luckily there wasn't one automobile on the street or someone might have been killed. Everyone was pretty shaken up, especially the motorman. He apologized and checked to make sure no one was hurt. It took a while to finally get straightened out and back on our way. We all thanked our lucky stars that no one was hurt.

44

The Studebaker

Upon Ray's graduation from Albright, he taught at Warwick High School in Knaurtown from September 1948 to May 1949. Since this was a distance from Reading he needed transportation so he bought a 1938 Studebaker. If I don't remember anything else about it I remember one thing; it had what is called a "hill hold." The car had a straight shift transmission; automatic transmissions were uncommon then. In most cars of this type, if you took your foot off the brake while traveling up a hill, the car drifted backwards.

However, Ray's car didn't drift backwards because of the hill hold feature. It had a ball and valve in the brake hydraulic system and as soon as the car started up an incline and you put your foot on the brake the ball rolled back and closed the valve, keeping the brake on even though you took your foot off of the brake. It would not release until the car started moving forward. That was really a big improvement over all other cars. I also remember that while Ray had the Studebaker, he took a course at night at Reading High School and overhauled the engine.

One Saturday I was outside washing the windows and Mother was in the cellar hanging up wash. The window I was washing had a broken rope that made it hard to move the window up and down. My hands were wet and soapy so when I tried to pull the top window down my right hand slipped off the bottom edge of the top window and went right through the glass of the bottom window. Glass shattered everywhere and when I looked down I noticed blood spurting out of my wrist and saw that one finger was cut pretty bad. I'm not sure whether I screamed or if just the noise brought everyone, but all of a sudden, there was Mrs. Schwartz with a clean towel to wrap around my wrist and pretty soon Ray showed up from I don't know where. We were lucky he had the Studebaker!

We were off to the hospital in a hurry and didn't even take time to tell our mother what happened. When we arrived in Emergency at the Community General Hospital there was no doctor available. The nurse had me sit in a chair with my head between my knees so that I wouldn't pass out. Finally, an intern showed up and he told us he was just wrapping up a little girl's arm and she was jiggling around so much that when he tried to cut the tape he cut her worse than she was before. I was about ready to leave then and go someplace else! However, he finally showed up and gave me ten stitches in my arm and finger.

That evening there was an article in the Reading Eagle newspaper. The headline of the article read, "Eludes Kamikaze, but window pane gets him."

45

Berkshire Knitting Mills

By the end of 1948, some of us machine erector apprentices had enough experience to move up to the next step in our training, which was to erect knitting machines at the Berkshire Knitting Mills. It was right next to the Textile Machine Works and was all part of the Wyomissing Industries. At that time it was the largest knitting mill in the world and consisted of seven or eight buildings and many of them were four stories high. At least two of those four story buildings had 42 knitting machines on each floor. They also had a dispensary there for the whole Wyomissing Industries with an ambulance and also a big dining hall for the employees.

We were transferred to the Berkshire to erect new knitting machines on floors where they had torn down obsolete ones. There were outside erectors and two men from Textile who were in charge of all the apprentices working at the Berkshire. Their names were Jim Brossman and Pete Mattis. They were both very nice and very good bosses. The outside erectors worked outside installing machines for other customers, and were temporarily installing machines at the Berkshire until another outside job came up. In the meantime, they were good experienced teachers for us apprentices. They put an apprentice with each of the experienced erectors to build a machine. If the erector got sent out before we finished the machine they put another experienced erector with us.

The big difference working at the Berkshire was that we were assembling machines that we had built at Textile. They were torn down and sent over to us and we put them up again. This time, however, we were responsible to finish the machine all the way so that it could knit. I experienced a sense of accomplishment once I finished the machine and saw it run making good stockings. Another big difference at the Berkshire was that every other machine was reversed so that they faced each other with an isle between. That way when they were finished and running, two knitters worked together running both machines.

One knitter was at each end of the isle and took care of both machines at his end. Also, at the Berkshire when an erector and an apprentice worked together, the erector built one machine and the apprentice built the other one. If they finished both machines the erector received 2/3 of the bonus and the apprentice got 1/3.

I met a lot of nice fellows at work and months later they put a Mexican fellow with me who was just a little older and was from a plant in Mexico. He was one of their mechanics and was sent to us to gain more experience. His first name was Frank and we became very good friends. Seven years later I was sent to Mexico City to erect some machines and we renewed old acquaintances.

A lot of the newer plants were air-conditioned and maintained a constant temperature. If the machine was built at a certain temperature it had to be run at that temperature. The Berkshire wasn't air-conditioned, but they maintained a certain temperature and humidity. It was pretty warm and humid all the time so it wasn't the best working conditions as far as comfort goes, but I got used to it.

The machines had to be set so close to maintain precision that a temperature change caused a problem. They found that after a machine ran about a half hour it built up so much heat that it changed everything and then there was trouble with it running right. So, we installed heating units with a heating wire that ran along the bed for the whole length of the machine. The heater was on the whole time we were building the machine and it put out about the same amount of heat that the machine builds up when it is running. A thermostat in the machine helped regulate an even temperature.

46

My First Car

While I was working at the Berkshire I decided to buy my first car... a green 1936 Plymouth. It had a straight round speedometer in the center of the dash and it used alcohol instead of permanent anti-freeze, so I had to be careful that it didn't boil over. It was a nice car, though, and it got me around pretty good. I had one little accident with it around the time I used to sing in the church choir. One Sunday afternoon the church choir decided to sing for the prisoners at the Berks County Prison. We went with the choir but Ray and I traveled to the prison in my Plymouth.

After the service was over and we were on our way I realized that we were the first people out and that if I hurried I could get turned around and be the first car out of the parking lot. Well, I hurried too much and when I backed up I didn't see a big stone and concrete post right behind me. I hit it dead center with my back bumper and put a v right in the center. Well, just about that time everyone was coming out just in time to see this happen. I was quite embarrassed and needless to say I think we were the last to leave!

When I worked at Berkshire, I looked forward to our regular breaks. We usually got a Coco-Cola out of the machine and in those days they were only five cents. About six of us had a little pool. Most of the glass Coco-Cola bottles had the name of the town printed on them indicating where they were bottled. So, every break, the fellow who got the bottle from the town that was the furthermost away received a nickel from the other five fellows.

That was fun.

47

The Navy Again???

I also found out around this time that some of the fellows I was working with had joined the active Navy Reserve. They went to meetings every month and got paid for it. When I got out of the Navy I wasn't a bit interested in the Reserves, but then I find out that some of the fellows were signing up for cruises and going to places like South America for two weeks in the summer. I got interested and decided to sign up in the inactive Reserve. That meant that I didn't have to go to meetings and didn't get paid but I still had the chance to go on a cruise. One time I put my name in for a cruise and they sent me a letter stating they didn't have any record of me being in the Navy. Well, a little over a year later the Korean Conflict broke out and they found my records in a hurry! They sent me a letter and gave me eight days to report for duty.

The Berkshire Knitting Mills was a beautiful place to work in the spring and summer. Between and around the buildings were red brick sidewalks and driveways with all kinds of trees, bushes and beautiful landscaping. There were a lot of cherry trees and when they were in bloom it was gorgeous. When the weather was nice everyone spent a lot of their lunchtime outside on the benches under the cherry trees or just walking around the grounds. When the weather wasn't nice we spent time in the cafeteria or in the big hall that they had for banquets and dances. There were plenty of tables and chairs where we could sit and listen to the good music played over the speaker system.

While Ray was going to Penn State he drove up on a Monday morning and usually came home on Friday afternoon or evening. About this time, we had a young couple with a little baby boy move in with us to help look after Mother and do the cooking. Their name was Frazer and they were from Baltimore. His name was James and the baby's name was James, but I don't remember her name. James was a student at Albright College and studying to be a minister. They were the nicest young couple. She cooked the meals and looked after Mother. I forget what the situation was, but I think they lived there for next to nothing, just for looking after our mother. We had them move in with us just in case I got sent out on the road while Ray was finishing his degree.

48

Guess Who I Met??

Since I had my own car now, I was able to run around a little more freely. I heard about a place where they taught dancing and then afterwards held a regular dance from 9 pm to Midnight. All this happened at Gundry's Dance Studio. It was run by Mr. & Mrs. Gundry and they taught ballroom dancing from eight until nine every Tuesday and Saturday evening. If you came for the lesson, you could also stay for the dance the rest of the evening for the same price. Some people however, just came for the dance.

The nice thing about it was that almost everyone came as a single and most of us were just learning to dance so everyone was pretty friendly and anxious to dance with each other for the practice. It was a great way to make new friends, especially of the opposite sex. I started going to Gundry's Dance Studio regularly on Tuesday and Saturday evenings and a few fellows from WPI came with me. We made a lot of friends with women, danced with most of them and had a lot of fun!

Then all of a sudden something happened. I met a certain girl at Gundry's and things haven't been the same since. She was an Irish girl and her name was Betty McBride. We danced a lot together and seemed to hit it off pretty good and soon I asked her for a date. She said yes and that was the start of something big. I met Betty around November and it was March that I asked her to marry me.

Also, sometime between November and March I got rid of the Plymouth and bought a nice dark blue two door Chevrolet. As I drove it off of the car lot the salesman said to me, "Be careful with this car, it has 100 horses under that hood." My Plymouth only had 60 horsepower.

We had a couple rough spots in between November and March but nothing we couldn't straighten out. I remember one Tuesday we went to Gundry's to the dance and Betty wanted to leave in the middle of it to go home and wash her hair in preparation for a date we had set up for the next night. I dropped her off at her house on Perkiomen Avenue and she said, "It's early yet, why don't you go back to the dance?" I told her I would go home and get to bed early. Well, on my way out I thought what the heck; it was pretty early and I decided to go back to the dance. I met one of my old dancing partners and we left together at the end of the dance.

The only problem was that when we left the dance, Elsie Banks was standing outside … and she happened to work with Betty at American Casualty. I knew right away that I might be in trouble and the following night I wished I had taken a sweater or coat with me. I could tell right away that Elsie must have told Betty about what she saw. We worked it out, though, but I think Betty thinks twice now before she tells me I can go and do something.

I am not quite sure how long the Frazers stayed with us on Pear Street but I think they may have left at the end of the summer of 1949. We were getting closer to the time that I would be finishing my trade and the way things looked there was a good chance that I might be sent out on a job somewhere on the road. We tried to find someone else who could live with our mother if I was sent away. Ray was still attending Penn State and he was planning to go to Millersville College. We finally found a lady through an agency. Her name was Edith and she moved in with our mother. They seemed to get along reasonably well.

Somewhere around August I finally gave Betty an engagement ring.

49

Wedding Bells!!

Betty and I had to make some decisions. I think that I was to finish my trade about October 15th and any time after that I could be sent away. We talked it over and all of a sudden we decided to get married the following weekend if we could arrange it! Betty had a minister friend whom she met in the Pocono's who pastored a church in Lima close to where she was living with her parents. This was another good reason for getting married soon. Her father, who worked for the telephone company was transferred to the Chester office somewhere around June and the family, including Betty, went with

him. I ran back and forth to Chester on weekends for quite some time.

The minister, Reverend Bill Sharp, said he would be glad to marry us, so Betty told her parents and her mother had a fit. Her mother wanted her to have a big wedding and I guess she preferred June. It was too sudden for her and she said she wasn't coming to the wedding and Betty said she would have it without her then.

We were married on October 8, 1949 at the Lima, PA Methodist Church where Reverend William Sharp officiated. My brother was the best man and Roma Fisher was the maid of honor. Betty's mother and father were both at the wedding but my mother couldn't make it because of her leg. Betty's mother had a dinner for all of us and we had wedding pictures taken by a photographer nearby. We went overnight on a honeymoon to Wilmington, Delaware and stayed at the Hotel DuPont. I had to be back to work in Reading on Monday morning.

I believe when Roma was maid of honor she and her boyfriend, Gordon Messler, asked Reverend Sharp if he would marry them on Thanksgiving and he agreed to do it.

I expected to be sent out on a new job soon after I was married so we decided not to set up housekeeping right away. Betty continued to live with her parents and I stayed in Reading where I was working. I kept running back and forth to Chester on weekends. We hoped it wouldn't be long but you know how that goes. Now that we were married they weren't sending anyone out on a job; at least that is the way it seemed.

50

Roma and Gordon's Wedding

While we were awaiting my transfer it wasn't long until Thanksgiving rolled around and Roma and Gordon got married. Betty was matron of honor and I was best man. They had a candlelight wedding at the Lima Methodist Church and

Reverend Sharp married them. It was a formal wedding and everyone was done up in lovely wedding dresses and tuxedoes. It was an interesting wedding to say the least. They rented a car for the wedding. It was a 1948 Chevrolet and had the new type of ignition switch that made it possible to put the ignition key into the switch and turn on the engine, then take the key out while the engine was still running and still turn the car off and on. I'm not sure if this was fortunate or not because...

Roma lived in Philadelphia and the wedding was in Lima about twenty miles away. She wanted to stop at the cemetery to place a wreath on her father's grave on the way to the church. As best man they asked me to drive the rented car. We couldn't find the key but were able to turn on the car anyway. Everyone was relieved and we were off to the cemetery. When we arrived Roma realized the wreath was locked in the trunk, which was impossible to open without the key. So,

she used Betty's spray of flowers instead and it was beautiful.

After that we went to the church and everything went according to plan. The reception was at Roma's house back in Philadelphia. I do seem to remember though that something happened later. Gordon changed his clothes to get ready to leave on his honeymoon when he realized that he mislaid his wallet. I think he and Roma were leaving for Washington and were going to stay at a Philadelphia hotel that first night. Ray thought that maybe he left his wallet in his tuxedo. Roma's uncle, who gave Roma away, had taken all of the tuxedo's to his home to return them the following Monday. Somehow Gordon eventually got his wallet before they left for Washington.

Shortly after the wedding I traded my 1940 Chevrolet in for a 1946 four door black or dark blue Chevrolet. I think I was looking ahead so that I would have room for everything when we left to go out on the road.

Week after week I drove down to Chester on weekends and I think a few times Betty stayed in Reading for a short time. We had a lot of fun on the weekends and liked to take short day trips. One time we went back down to Wilmington to see the play Harvey. I believe Joe E. Brown played in it. Another time we went up to Allentown and stayed at the hotel Tremore. We also drove down to Atlantic City the last day of the year and spent New Year's Eve at a motel.

I'm happy we had the chance to do all those things because it wasn't long until I got my orders to leave. If I remember correctly, my boss called me in and asked me if I could leave by Friday for Franklin, North Carolina. I told him I was ready to leave anytime.

Since we were newlyweds and hadn't set up housekeeping we had to buy a lot of things to get started. I was a little short on cash at the time so I asked my new boss if they would forward me a little money until my next pay. He said yes and that I should go up to the payroll department where they would give me $100 in advance. I was grateful they agreed to allow me to pay it back slowly and we were greatly relieved. We packed up and left for Franklin the first week in January of 1950.

51

Franklin, NC

Betty and I loaded our car with clothing and wedding presents and left on Friday, so that we would be there in time for me to start work the following Monday. If we elected to drive down to Franklin, I was allowed to submit traveling expenses. The company paid expenses equal to first class Pullman fare on the train for both of us as well as the amount it would cost to send my tools and baggage. They also gave me eight hours a day wages while we were traveling.

It was about 600 miles from Chester to Franklin over a lot of narrow roads that wound around the mountains of North Carolina. Some of the roads looped around so many times that we almost thought we would meet ourselves coming around the other side! We discovered that Franklin was in the Smoky Mountains and that all roads into Franklin went up over the mountains. It was a little overwhelming to drive on the winding roads with no guardrails…because it was a long way down.

We arrived in Franklin late in the afternoon on Saturday just in time to find a motel before dark. It wasn't a motel like we are accustomed to today with 100 rooms or more. It was a motel with about five or six cabins and an office, and after all that driving it felt pretty good to settle in for the night. Initially, we weren't very impressed with the small town of Franklin, its population of 2,000 and its main street that was only 4 blocks long. However, after living there for a short time we learned to love it.

My boss told me before I left that I would be working with an

 erector by the name of Sam McPherson. He was the boss and we were going to build a machine side by side. Well, this worked out great except that when we finished the machines he received 2/3 of the bonus and I got 1/3.

On Sunday we started looking for Sam McPherson as well as for a place to stay. I think we found Sam first. He also had just arrived in Franklin, pulling a 28 foot trailer with a wife and two children. His wife's name was Peg and they had a daughter, Peggy and a son, Sammy. I soon found out his wife was from Reading and I believe that she graduated from Reading High School the same year as my brother. We found them at a small trailer court right outside of town. It's bad enough driving those mountain roads into Franklin but imagine pulling a 28-foot trailer!

I think we checked in at the plant on Monday morning but then Betty and I went looking for a place to live. We found an apartment with an old couple right on Main Street. He was the retired Postmaster in town and the apartment was on the second floor. It only had one or two rooms and was thirty dollars a month. I paid the thirty dollars in advance, but after the first night we decided to move because we discovered there were roaches all over the place. Sadly, I didn't get my thirty dollars back.

The next day we started looking again and found another apartment a couple blocks away. It was on the second floor and it looked nicer but when we saw that they hung all their hams up there to cure, we decided not to take the chance. Finally we got lucky and found a nice basement apartment on a corner property on the main street on the edge of town. It was a brick home and the landlady, Mrs. Leach, had several tenants. One was the Mayor of a little town in Georgia who lived there with his wife. Mrs. Leach's daughter and grandson also had an apartment. We had one of the two basement units and it was great. It was a kitchen, bathroom and bath and clean. I also could park my car in the rear of the building.

Once we got settled, Sam and I got started at work. The name of the place was Van Raalte and it was a nice clean, modern air-conditioned plant and the people were welcoming and friendly. They had about twelve machines and they were buying six more. Sam and I were going to build them.

131

52

Send More Money

We stayed in the first apartment for a week and then moved into Mrs. Leach's apartment. Her apartment was $45 a month and since I didn't get any of the $30 back we were short on cash. I had figured that my first pay in Franklin would be about $110 but instead it was $10! They had taken out the entire $100 loan the first week instead of a little at a time like they had promised. I didn't like this at all. I went right over to the telegraph office and sent my boss a telegram, "Send more money."

The next morning I received a telegraph money order for $200. The first thing on Monday morning the secretary from the office came out to me and told me that my boss was on the phone and that he wanted to talk to me. When I answered the phone he started yelling at me, "You asked for money before you left and as soon as you get there you send me a message asking for more money? What the hell's going on down there?" All I said to him was, "Yes, and my first pay was $10." He replied, "Oh those dumb SOB's, don't worry about it, I'll take care of it" and hung up. It was about a month until they took any money out of my pay. I don't think my boss ever forgot me after that.

Soon after I started working I met one of the employees who lived on a farm and his dog had just had puppies. He offered me one and we decided to take it. It was a male dog and loaded with fleas. We called him "Butch" and he went just about everywhere we went. He was our first dog and we trained him well even though we spoiled him. He was some kind of a terrier. The first night he kept us up half the night. He felt bad because he was taken from his

mother and had trouble settling down to rest. Then someone told us to put an alarm clock in his bed with him and that did the trick. He slept fine after that and so did we.

Sam and I got along very well and I enjoyed working with him and working at Van Raalte. Betty and Sam's wife, Peg, got along well also and spent a lot of time together while we were working. In fact, Betty decided she wanted to learn how to drive. So I started to teach her after she got her learner's permit and Peg rode with her when she wanted to get some practice. I didn't envy Peg riding with her all over the countryside and on those mountain roads without any guardrails. But she persevered, and she finally got her driver's license.

A sad but funny thing happened when she passed her test. She decided to drive to Van Raalte to pick me up at work because she was so happy and proud that she passed. There were only about two cars on the lot and she parked next to one of them, and she hit it. It was only a scratch but I think it was a new car and the fellow wasn't too happy.

We really loved Franklin. I was getting paid $45 a week for living expenses, which covered all the necessities plus the entire running around we did acting like tourists. My regular pay was being deposited at home. I was working ten hours a day, five days a week, and on weekends we acted like tourists gallivanting to wherever we wanted to go. We traveled all around the Smokey Mountains, visited all the tourist traps and any other place that caught our interest. We really had a ball. There was a 6,000-foot mountain peak that we liked to drive up. It was called Wyah Bald and had a great view. Other weekends we visited many towns around Franklin as well. They were all small towns, just like Franklin but each one had something different to offer and most of them were about 20 or 30 miles away.

Seventy miles northeast of Franklin we discovered the town of Asheville. Actually, I guess it was big enough to be called a city! We lived in Macon County, which was a "dry" county. In other words we could not buy any beer or liquor in Franklin or the whole county of Macon. If we wanted beer we had to drive to the Georgia border,  which was about fifteen miles away where there was a gas station that sold beer. For liquor we had to drive all the way to Asheville.

Soon after we arrived in Franklin we heard a story about an undertaker who threw a party at his home and most everyone was invited. Evidently this was common practice down south. The story went that every Thursday or Friday he drove over to Asheville with his hearse and loaded up with booze. I don't know how true this was because we never tried to go to the party!

A Good Time to Have a Friend

While working at Van Raalte I became friends with the mechanic who took care of their equipment. His name was John Cogan and Betty became friends with his wife, Caroline. Sometimes we visited each other or went out together. After paying for some car repairs, the four of us decided to go to Asheville for the day. We got all dressed up and went and had a nice dinner there. Even though we could buy liquor in Asheville they did not serve it in the restaurant. So we took the liquor with us in a brown paper bag and kept it under the table. They sold us the set ups, which consisted of glasses and ice cubes along with whatever we wanted to mix with our drinks. We had a real nice time together and headed home to Franklin pretty late.

We had seventy miles of mountain roads to travel. About half way home as we were coming up this real big hill and all of a sudden the engine started to run rough and lose power. I finally had to stop. Luckily I had some tools in the trunk and better yet John knew quite bit about car engines. He determined that the valves had to be reset. He said they were set a little too close when they rebuilt my engine so he took the valve cover off and readjusted the valves right there on the side of that lonely road. Half an hour later we were off and running and everything was fine. I sure was glad that he was along that night.

Weekend Tourists

Clayton, Georgia was right over the border where we could buy beer at the gas station. When we took the road to a little town called The Highlands, we drove under a waterfall called Bridal Veil Falls. It was amazing. The road to Murphy eventually took us to the desolate town of Copper Hill. Nothing grew there and the ground had a copper color due to something they mined. The road to Bryson City led to Newfound Gap, and then Gatlinburg, a famous tourist trap with lots of shops and motels. These places were all in the middle of the Great Smoky Mountains National Park. It also was across the border into Tennessee. Not far from there we ventured to the Cherokee Indian Reservation. That was a beautiful area to see. We saw a suspension bridge that we could walk on. It was made of rope and wooden boards.

In April, Betty and I, with the McPherson family, had a picnic at the Fontana Dam in Tennessee. There was a nice park right there and tours were given through the dam. We never took any advertised tours. On weekends we just enjoyed taking a different road out of town and seeing where it went and what was there.

The Sylvia road eventually led to Asheville and one time Mrs. Leach took us to a mica mine. At the entrance to the mine, if you bought a ticket, you could go into the mine with a bucket and dig up one bucket of ground and then look through it to see what you came up with. I don't know what we expected to find, but we didn't find anything unusual.

While we lived in Franklin the Cherokee Indian Reservation produced a beautiful play every year called, "Come Unto These Hills." We went with Mrs. Leach and her daughter and attended the opening show July 1, 1950. To this day, the play goes on!

Another weekend Betty and I took a ride over to Knoxville, Tennessee and stayed overnight at a motel. We also took a tour of the Oak Ridge Atomic Energy Plant and that was interesting.

We lived in Franklin at a nice time, as far as the weather went. When we left Pennsylvania it was very cold but when we arrived in Franklin it was shirtsleeve weather. After living there for a while, we discovered we could drive up in the mountains and enjoyed making snowmen and then come back to Franklin where it was nice and warm.

It didn't take long for us to also find there were a lot of craft people, skilled carpenters and cabinetmakers living in the area. We found a good cabinetmaker and he made us a table to our specifications. His name was Mr. Purdom and he lived on Wayah Road. We wanted a table that had a place for books, a shelf for magazines, plus an area to place our table radio upon. When we explained to him what we wanted, he drew up a blueprint and made it. He used cherry wood and it turned out great. We were very pleased.

The downtown shopping area was only four blocks long and included one movie theater, a small hospital, a Western Auto Store, a 5&10 cent store, a few clothing stores, and a hardware store. On Saturdays we had to be pretty careful when we walked down the main street because all the farmers came to town and most of them chewed tobacco "cuds." They liked to lean back against the storefront and spit out to the curb and you hoped that you weren't walking by at the time!

55

The Law

Franklin was the county seat of Macon County with a courthouse in the square. It must have been built about 1870 and when we went inside we saw where everybody had missed the spittoons over the years!

A funny thing happened at the end of our first month in Franklin. I drove by the courthouse to go to work from our apartment. Most of the time I went home for lunch, which meant I drove past the courthouse twice at lunchtime. It so happened that my car had what they called a Holiday Muffler. When I stepped on the gas pretty hard it made a real nice noise. The problem was these mufflers were illegal in Franklin and most of the time the State Police, who had their office in the court house, sat outside on a bench during lunch time.

So, every day as I drove by I took my foot off the gas and sort of coasted by the courthouse. As I did this they watched me go by as if they were waiting for me. My good fortune lasted for a little while. I will never forget the day I approached the courthouse and one of the cops got off of his bench and walked out to the center of the road and put his hand up to stop me. When I stopped he walked over to me and said, "You better have North Carolina license plates on your car." I thanked him and slowly drove off without making much noise.

The law was that after you live in a different state for more than 30 days you had to get a license of that state as well as change the driver's license. There wasn't any problem getting a North Carolina license plate. All I did was go into the Western Auto Store and asked for a new one. I filled out a form, paid them and they gave me a new license plate right away. Getting a driver's license, however, took a little longer because I had to go to the State Police for that.

Police officers in our county drove silver 1950 Buicks and the State Police in the next county in Sylva received a fleet of new 1950 Fords. One day one of the State Police from each of the counties decided to see which car was the fastest. The bad part was that they decided to race down the winding narrow mountain road between Sylva and Franklin. As you can imagine, one of them didn't make it around one of the curves and went down over the side of the mountain.

He didn't get killed but he totaled the car. I think they both were fired after that.

56

Visiting and Visitors

My company had a rule that if we wanted to we could work extra time and save it for later. In other words, if we wanted to work 50 hours a week and only turn in 45 hours and save the other 5 hours we were allowed to do that. Then we would be paid for 45 hours a week. At the end of each week we filled out a time sheet and had the plant manager sign and verify it and then we mailed it to Textile Machine Works who sent us our checks.

If we saved time each week we let the plant manager know about it and once we accumulated two weeks' time, he validated the timesheets and we either took a vacation around the area or went home for one to two weeks. If we decided to go home we usually did it at the end of three months and the company paid for our transportation back and forth. Because of this policy, we were able to return home twice and always went by automobile.

The last week in June, Betty's parents came down to Franklin for a visit. They took the train and we picked them in Greensboro. They stayed with two elderly women who had a boarding house right across the street from where we lived and we kept busy showing them all of the sights in the area. We had a great time together and I think they were glad they made the trip.

57

Moving On

What is the saying, "All good things come to an end?" Well Sam and I finally finished our job and so it was time to move on to our next job in Burlington, North Carolina. We had enough time to go home to Pennsylvania for a visit and then proceed to Burlington. Not too long before this I ran across a homemade wooden luggage trailer on sale for $40. It seemed very sturdy and had a California license plate on the back. Evidently, someone built it in California and pulled it to North Carolina so I thought it must be pretty good.

So, I bought it, got a license for it and now we had a little more room to carry what we had accumulated while living in Franklin. I also ordered a tarpaulin from Sears & Roebuck mail order so that I had something to cover everything in the trailer. Somehow the order got mixed up with someone's order from Florida and they sent me a bigger tarpaulin than the one I ordered. I called Sears and they said that if I was satisfied I could keep it. I was pleased because it worked out very well.

We made a lot of very nice friends in Franklin but now it was time to say goodbye. We left for Pennsylvania around the middle of July pulling our luggage trailer, which was pretty well loaded up. Before we left I practiced driving around with it, especially backing up which is an art in itself.

On the trip I had to keep reminding myself that I was pulling a trailer. Now and then I forgot about the trailer and one time I missed a turn so I just swung into a gas station and almost wiped out the pumps! Luckily, I stopped just in time. Later while traveling on a narrow and winding road during a rainstorm, we came upon a place where all the traffic was pulled over to the side of the road. I guess I didn't question why they were pulled over because I just kept going past all of them only to discover a big mudslide that closed the road. There wasn't room to turn around, so, guess what? I had to back up all that distance and it was a long line. At that point I found out that backing up straight is about the hardest thing you can be asked to do.

I took it slow and easy and we were eventually at the end of the line. Soon after a big tractor trailer truck pulled up and I started talking to him. He was in a hurry and said he knew of another road over the mountain and that if he could get turned around he was going to try it. I waited to see if he could and when he did I thought I might as well try it also. I managed to get turned around without much trouble and followed him all the way out of North Carolina. By the time I got home I felt like I was an experienced driver pulling trailers!

We stayed with Betty's parents in Chester while we were in Pennsylvania and enjoyed a short visit to my mother in Reading. We also visited some friends in Philadelphia and as we drove up Roosevelt Boulevard a policeman stepped out in the road and motioned for me to stop. He pointed to my inspection sticker in the corner of my windshield and asked me if I knew that it had run out. I said to him, "Have you looked at my license plates?" When he saw that they were North Carolina plates he got a little embarrassed and told me to get rid of that old Pennsylvania sticker and then he let us go. It turned out that the old Pennsylvania sticker expired the day before and he was standing there looking for any old stickers to go by. He didn't realize that I was from out of state and that North Carolina doesn't have inspection stickers.

58

Close Call

We left for Burlington pulling our trailer loaded with everything we owned. Since Burlington is in the eastern part of the state, we were able to go down the eastern shore highway to Cape Charles and then take the Cape Charles Ferry to Norfolk, Virginia. It was about a two hour ferry ride.

While driving down the eastern shore highway, a big dog suddenly ran out right in front of us. I had been traveling about 50 miles an hour and I was still pulling the luggage trailer. As I hit the break, the car slowed down momentarily and then continued on. I realized I had brushed the dog without hurting it but after that I had no breaks. I gradually was able to slow down enough to put the hand brake on as I pulled off the road.

After inspecting our car, I discovered that the weight of the trailer caused the back of the car to ride low enough to rub on the hydraulic brake line and wear it thin enough that when I hit the brake so hard, it ruptured the brake line. It held just long enough that I didn't hurt the dog. If the line hadn't broken and my brakes had held I might have skidded or the trailer might have jackknifed and caused a bad accident. I always felt that somebody was looking over us.

At that point I decided to drive slowly into the next town that was only a few miles away. I was able to use my hand brake and we made it into the next town of Kiptopeke. I found a garage that was preparing to close for the day but was able to talk them into working on my car before they went home. They replaced the brake line and had me on my way within about a half hour.

However, as soon as I got out of town, I discovered that something else wasn't right. I think they didn't bleed the air out of the lines because the brake pedal felt very spongy. It wasn't long before I had very little brake again. I continued to carefully push on through and after another ten or fifteen miles, we reached the town of Cape Charles. I was able to find a garage that was just closing and they said that I could leave my car there and they would look at it the first thing on the morning. I agreed and then we went on to find a motel nearby.

After a good breakfast the next morning, we walked down the street to the garage. We had our dog Butch on a lead and all of a sudden, out of nowhere, a big black cat jumped right on to Butch's back. He let out a yelp and we somehow chased the cat away but it scared us half to death. Butch wasn't too happy about it either!

When we arrived at the garage they had everything taken care of and we soon were on our way to the ferry that was just out of town. The ferry

was just pulling into the dock when we arrived at the landing. There was a long line of cars waiting for the ferry and we were stuck at the end of it. While we were waiting the ticket man came along and sold us a ticket. The fare was $3.60 and I handed the ticket to Betty to hold onto. We sat there quite a while talking about what happened to us the day before.

Finally, the cars started to move and as we drove onto the ferry we stopped for man standing at the entrance collecting tickets. I reached over to Betty for the ticket and she handed me a handful of little pieces of paper! While we were talking, she tore up the ticket into little pieces without realizing what she had done. I took the handful of paper and handed it over to the ticket collector and drove on to the ferry. I'm not sure what he said but he sure had a surprised look on his face. The Chesapeake Bay tunnel has since replaced this ferry.

59

Burlington

We arrived in Burlington late afternoon and we met up with the McPherson family. I'm not sure if we had planned to meet or if it was accidental, but I remember that we sat around outside. Sam was sitting on the ground and, all of a sudden, Butch went over to him, lifted his leg and tinkled all over Sam's leg. I guess Butch was happy to see him.

Betty and I stayed at a tourist home the first couple days and then Sam's mother offered to let us stay with her. She had a home a few miles out of Burlington with some land around it. Sam put his trailer on her land and they lived in it there. She gave us the upstairs in her home. It had a nice big room and she gave us the use of the kitchen. Most of the time she had coffee, corn bread or biscuits waiting for us when we woke up. We called her Granny and she was real nice to us. We moved into her place August 9, 1950.

Tower Hosiery was a larger plant than Van Rialto but it was a clean plant and the people seemed very friendly. Sam and I started working there on August 7, 1950. We were supposed to build four machines.

Burlington was a medium size town, much bigger than Franklin. I guess we were spoiled living in the Smoky Mountains because it took a while to adjust to living in a more populated area with a lot of flat tobacco farmland.

One night after we moved into Granny's house, Betty and I had just gone to bed and were making love when I felt something over our bed. I turned the light on and there was a bat flying around in the room. We pulled the covers up and ducked underneath hoping it would go away but it didn't. I sprung from the bed to try to catch the bat... I guess I made a pretty picture running around without any clothes on. The good news is I finally caught the bat!

60

Almost a DeSoto!!

On August 25, 1950, Betty and I went to look at a 1950 DeSoto in one of the car lots. It was either brand new or it only had a couple thousand miles on it, but I liked it very much. It was too late in the evening to buy the car because the bank was closed but the salesman offered to loan us the car for the weekend so we could see how we liked it. He filled the gas tank and said we could get the paperwork straightened out on Monday when the banks reopened. We took him up on his offer and drove it to Atlanta for the weekend. It was a pretty long trip and we decided that we really wanted to buy the car.

Monday morning I went to work with the idea that after work I would go down to the car dealer and trade the Chevrolet in on the DeSoto. At about 9 o'clock in the morning the secretary from the front office come out to tell me that there was a registered letter for me down at the post office.

At noon I went down to the post office to get the letter and to my surprise it was "Greetings." I had orders to report to Philadelphia on September 6th for active duty in the Navy. Here, I thought there was no record of me being in the Navy. But when the Korean Conflict broke out they found my records in a hurry! I immediately went down to the car dealer, showed him my letter and told him I wanted my Chevrolet back. Fortunately, they still had it. They weren't very happy to take the Desoto back, especially with an empty gas tank, but they knew they didn't have much choice. If I kept it I wouldn't have had to pay too much on it until I got back out of the Navy.

61
Heading Home

I headed back to work with my Chevrolet to tell them the news, and when I returned to Granny's house I told Betty. We packed, said our goodbyes to everyone and we were on our way home that evening. We went through Washington, D.C. about two in the morning and arriving in Chester at dawn.

You can imagine that this came as a big shock to everyone including me. I had a lot of things to get straightened out and only about a week to do it. We went home to Reading to see my mother and my brother. I found out that Ray had sent a letter to the Commandant of the 5th Naval District requesting that I not be recalled because of a hardship, the need to support our mother.

We soon received a letter back. It read, "Request denied. Report as ordered."

That week went by in a hurry and after saying goodbye to everyone I was ready to leave. We spent our last night in Chester with Betty's parents.

Part IV

62

Philadelphia Navy Yard

On the way to the Navy Yard the next morning, I had a flat tire and fortunately, I had time to change it and walk through the gate at Noon, just on time.

You can't possibly imagine the feeling I had as I walked back into the Navy Yard and reported for duty. I was thinking about eleven months ago when Betty and I were married and moved to North Carolina, where I was supposed to be working instead of returning to the Navy. It was one of the worst days of my life. It also was a bad day for Betty.

With that part of my life behind me, I left Betty, my car and our dog Butch standing at the gate of the Philadelphia Navy Yard not knowing when I would see them again. I found out where I was supposed to check in and spent the afternoon getting a physical and receiving all my clothing and uniforms. I was assigned a bunk in one of the barracks and then the Chief Petty Officer told me to check the watch list and duty roster. After doing so I discovered that I had the mid watch as a fire watch walking around the outside of the barracks from midnight until 0400. I also found out that the next day I was assigned to a working party on the aircraft carrier USS Monterey.

Then it really hit me. I thought to myself, "What the hell am I doing back here?" I guess it was my own fault. I did sign up for the Reserves and this is what I got. It seems as if the government was panicking a little bit. I was considered to have a critical rating, which is why I was called back, but there weren't any submarines out there. They didn't seem to be turning anyone down. The fellow behind me in line had only one hand and a hook for the other hand, but they took him. Another fellow was married, had three children, and his wife was expecting another child soon, but they still took him. They said that when she had the baby he could go home.

63

Working Party

The next day I was sent with the working party to the aircraft carrier Monterey. As soon as I stepped on the deck I saw Lieutenant Marcus. He had been our commissary officer on the USS Loy and was just an Ensign at that time. It just so happened that he was the officer who tried to have me court-martialed for working against the best interest of the ship. So, he wasn't exactly on the top of my list, but there he was.

He saw me first and he came running over to me with outstretched arms, like a long lost brother. He invited me into his stateroom and we sat down and talked for a long time. I guess I shouldn't complain because I was supposed to be working on a working party. He told me that he also was in the Reserves and that he had been called back into the Navy. When he first received his letter he wrote back to them telling them that he was sorry but he couldn't make it because his wife was pregnant. They sent him another letter saying that he better make it or else.

I found out later that his wife had a baby and he did get out. He was pretty good at doing things like that. While we were on the Loy, as soon as he heard that we were going to the Pacific, he got a transfer off of the ship right before we went through the Panama Canal. Anyway, I talked to him quite a while and then got to work with my working party. I believe our job was loading ship stores. We were all under quarantine the first week for 10 days. All I could do in the beginning was talk to Betty on the phone in the evening. Eventually, she was able to come on the base at night where we went to the movies together.

As soon as I received my notice to go back in the Navy, Betty and I had a few long talks about what we wanted to do as far as planning for the future. She wanted to try to become pregnant and have a child even with the possibility that there was a chance I wouldn't come back. She said that at least she would have a part of me then. We did decide to take that path even though there were not a lot of opportunities to do anything about it!

I stayed at the Philadelphia Navy Yard a little over two weeks and in that time Betty came to visit me at the base whenever she was allowed. Right before I got my orders to leave Philadelphia I was able to go home to Chester overnight maybe two or three times.

64

On Our Way!!!

I found out we were leaving for San Francisco the next day by train. I don't think I was able to see Betty again before we left though. I was, however, able to talk to her on the phone and tell her when we were leaving the Philadelphia station. She said she would be sitting on the hood of our car at the railroad crossing in Chester so we might catch a glimpse of each other. She told me she would be wearing a bright red dress with Butch at her side!

The troop train left the Philadelphia station loaded with sailors. It was late morning September 21. As we approached Chester I started to look for Betty and Butch. Sure enough, as the train passed where she said she would be, I saw the car parked along the side of the tracks with Betty sitting on the hood with Butch and she was waving and of course a few thousand sailors were waving back at her! She told me later that there were so many sailors that she just started waving when the train got there and kept waving until it was all passed. I guess she never did actually see me.

The train consisted of Pullman cars and a couple dining cars and we all had beds to sleep in at night, so that made the trip more enjoyable. After Chester, we went through Baltimore, Washington, West Virginia, Ohio, Indiana, Illinois, and then Missouri on the B & O railroad.

Traveling across country was nice most of the time, but when every mile takes you farther away from home and the one you love, it doesn't feel very good. It puts a bad feeling in your stomach knowing that you probably won't be home again for a long time, if ever. I guess that was an all-time low in my life but fortunately I was able to see it through and keep looking forward to the time that I would be coming home again.

I guess I did a lot of looking out the window. There certainly was plenty to see in an ever changing countryside. I also did a lot of reading and we played a lot of pinochle.

In St. Louis we changed to the Missouri & Pacific railroad although we kept the same Pullman cars the whole trip. This took a lot of moving cars around in the railroad yards and they said it would take some time so they told us we could get off the train and go into town for a little while. I believe they gave us an hour or so. The station seemed to be right in downtown St. Louis so some of us took off and walked uptown.

We eventually stopped at a bar to have a drink and while we were there we met three nice young couples. They were very friendly and asked us where we were going and we told them that we were waiting for our train to be made up. They left and said they would come down to the station to wave us goodbye. We stayed at the bar a little longer until we realized we had to hurry so that we didn't miss our train.

As we were running through the station, all of a sudden, we heard someone yelling goodbye. We looked around and saw the three couples we had met earlier. They actually did come down to the station to wave goodbye. We didn't have time to stop and talk, but we waved to them as we were getting on the train. It probably was just the uniform we had on but it gave us a good feeling to know somebody cared about us a little bit when we were so far from home.

We went on to Kansas City, Missouri where we were transferred to the Union Pacific railroad for the rest of the trip. They say that from Kansas City on there is a gradual upgrade, although you would never know it. The land looked so flat.

Our next state was Colorado and we were scheduled to pull into Denver sometime around four in the afternoon. That was where I hoped to mail the letter I wrote to Betty.

In Denver we headed north and went through Wyoming and over through Salt Lake, Utah, Reno, Nevada and then into California. It was quite a train ride but it got awful monotonous. I read newspapers, 25 cent novels and did quite a bit of sleeping. Some of the fellows played poker but I wasn't tempted. I was down to $7 and didn't want to lose it foolishly. At every meal they passed a dish around for a tip for the stewards and we are expected to put in about 20 or 25 cents. That slowly drained my spending money.

We had an extra stop in Sparks, Nevada because we were developing a flat wheel and I guess it was causing a vibration. I don't know what they had to do but they fixed it and we were able to get off the train and stretch our legs a little bit. We were expected to be in San Francisco by about six the next morning. They said we would have to get up at five in the morning and be ready to leave the train when we pulled into the station. We had another tiresome day of riding and we stopped at Ogden, Utah and picked up some more cars, including another dining car. We had turkey for dinner and had been getting good meals!

65

San Francisco

On Tuesday, September 26, 1950 we arrived in San Francisco early in the morning. We were taken out to the naval base on Treasure Island and set up in barracks. We got another physical, dental examination and bag inspection and were scheduled for an Admiral's inspection the next day. They announced that anyone who gave a pint of blood would be exempt from the Admiral's inspection and would get weekend liberty. They got so many volunteers that I decided to keep my blood a little longer.

The best part of my day was that I got two letters from Betty. They were the first letters since I left Philadelphia. In her letter she said she was late with her period, so we kept our fingers crossed. I called my cousin Walter Herner who lived in San Mateo and he invited me to their house. He and his wife Ruth, and two children, and his father William, my uncle, all lived in a house in San Mateo twenty miles south of San Francisco. He told me how to get there and I went that night. I took a train and him and Ruth met me at the station. They had a nice home and it was good to see my uncle again. I hadn't seen any of them since before World War Two. I enjoyed a nice visit and they invited me to come back on Sunday for a turkey dinner and he promised to show me around a little bit.

For the next few days I had a rough schedule. We were up out of bed by 0600, got washed and dressed and headed right into the chow line to wait about an hour to an hour and a half. At 0800 we fell in for muster and stood there about an hour for announcements, roll call, etc. At 1000 the mail line opened and we stood for about another hour. By that time it was time for chow so we got in that line and waited almost two hours! Sometimes I went back to the barracks and wrote letters for an hour before I got in line. We had muster again at 1300 and stood around again for a while. Then, of course, if you were interested in getting mail, you had to get back in the mail line at about 1500. Well, so much for that…that was enough waiting for one war!

They had movies on the base at night for 12 cents so I went to see a couple of them. Besides visiting my cousin, I went on liberty one night into San Francisco. I found out that it was a long drag into San Francisco from Treasure Island. First, we took a Navy bus across the island to the gate where we got off the bus until the marine guard checked everyone's identification card. We then got back on the bus that took us to the Oakland Bay Bridge and then took the train into San Francisco. It was much like the elevated in Philadelphia. Overall, the trip took a good 45 minutes.

On Friday, September 29 we had the Admiral's inspection. We mustered at 1300 in our dress blue uniform, clean hats, polished shoes, etc. and then stood and waited for the inspection, which was at 1500. About 1,000 of us paraded out on the drill field and marched in review past the Admiral. Everyone was all polished up, officers with their kid gloves, flag bearers and a big brass band to march with. It really looked good with everyone marching in step to the music. It was one of those times that made you feel patriotic and good to be in the Navy. Ha! Ha! Ha! That's a good one.

On Saturday, September 30 they posted another draft list and I was on it! We were to fly out the next evening and I was assigned to the USS Mansfield DD 728. I found out that it was off of the western coast of Korea in the invasion of Inchon. As soon as I got a chance, I called my cousin to let him know that I wouldn't be able to make Sunday dinner. I was really disappointed.

On Sunday October 1st we flew out of the Moffet Air Base at 2215 on a big four-engine marine transport plane. That was the first time I had ever flown and I wasn't very happy to be leaving late at night, in the dark, heading out over the Pacific Ocean. On top of that we were seated in one long row down each side of the plane facing each other on a piece of canvas stretched over three metal rods for seats. In the center of the plane were a couple big spare engines strapped down to the deck. To top it all off they give us life jackets with ditching instructions, in case we had to land in the ocean!

66

Hawaii

It took 12 hours for our flight and we finally landed in Honolulu, Hawaii. We stayed at an airfield about 30 miles from Honolulu and were told that we were definitely going to Japan. It was nice and warm in Hawaii even though the trip over was cold. We flew at 9,000 feet and the plane wasn't heated much. We all wore our pea coats but our legs froze. We stayed for two or three days because we had #2 priority where anyone with # 1 priority flew out the same day.

Do you remember me telling you that there was a fellow who came back in the Navy when I did and he had a wife, three children and they were expecting another one any day? Well, when we got off the plane they told him she had a baby and that he could go home! He was a very happy man!

Johnson Island

By Thursday October 5 I was on my way again. They posted the list and I was on it. Bob Hope and his troop arrived that day for a show for the servicemen and we missed it. He was on his way to Korea and Japan, so we hoped we would get a chance to see them later.

We took off at 2000 and at midnight we landed on a tiny little island called Johnson Island. It was so small that when we landed the wheels of the plane touched the water and when we stopped at the end of the runway the wheels were in the water again. When we taxied up to the hanger a sign read, "Welcome to Johnson Island, 234 people and three dogs." We ate a hot meal there and took off again in about an hour.

Kwajalein

On the way to Kwajalein we smelled gasoline but they couldn't seem to find the leak. So, they told everyone not to smoke cigarettes until we landed. It was about an eight-hour flight and we arrived there at about 8 o'clock Saturday morning. We only had four hours of Friday and then we crossed the International Date Line, and it became Saturday. We got off the plane and they took us to a mess hall for breakfast. The mechanics continued to look for the gas leak while some of the people in the mess hall told us about the plane of Navy nurses that crashed there last week. They said that when the plane of nurses arrived a week ago they complained of smelling gasoline and they thought that they might have a gas leak.

They never found it and took off. As they leveled out at 9,000 feet it blew up and all 40 nurses were killed. Well, that sure made us feel good!! It seemed as if we had the same problem. We stayed there an hour and a half to have breakfast and up to that time they hadn't found any gas leak. So, we took off and headed for Guam.

It was another eight hour flight, and as we approached Guam our one engine started to throw oil and it started to smoke. We made an emergency landing with all the fire trucks there and everything, but we landed safely. We stayed there all day while they worked on the engine and about 11 o'clock that night they decided that it was probably safe to take off. We took off after that and headed for Tokyo, Japan. We arrived in Tokyo on Sunday, October 8, our first wedding anniversary.

67

Tokyo, Japan
Sunday, October 8th
(Our first wedding anniversary)

After forty hours of flying we finally made it to Japan! I figured since I left Philadelphia I was at least 10,000 miles from home. We landed at the Hadena airfield at 0700. Then a bus took us from the airport to the Naval Receiving Station in Yokosuka, Japan that was a good half hour from Tokyo. It was formerly the Japanese Yokosuka Naval Base. We checked into a barrack, ate breakfast and then, after having to do exactly nothing all morning, we had dinner. When we went into the mess hall everything was already placed on the table, family style. We just had to sit down and start eating. If we ran out of anything there was always a Japanese waiter standing by to fill the dish. After dinner I was able to get a haircut from a Japanese barber and also a shoeshine...all for free.

We didn't stay very long and by five o'clock that evening we left for the railroad station to take the train to Sasebo, Japan and it was a 36- hour ride!

Sasebo, Japan: USS Mansfield

On Tuesday October 10, our train arrived in Sasebo, Japan early in the morning. I reported aboard the USS Mansfield about 0900 and she had recently arrived in Sasebo. She had been in the Inchon invasion when she hit a mine, had about 30 casualties and was pretty banged up. She had most of her bow blown off and with all of this damage there wasn't enough room for all of the crew to sleep. Some of us temporarily moved over on the USS Dixie until repairs were made.

The Mansfield expected to be in Sasebo three to four weeks for repairs and then she was going back to the United States for a complete overhaul. I thought it would be great if I could go along back with them, but of course that was wishful thinking. There was already is a rumor that about 70 men of the crew were going to transferred before they left.

Our trip by train from Yokosuka to Sasebo was rather nice. It took us about 36 hours and we traveled by coach during the day and Pullman at night. It gave us a good chance to get a look at Japan. We passed through Kobe, Osaka, Hiroshima, and Nagasaki. The last two places were the two cities hit by the atomic bomb. From what we had seen so far of Japan, it wasn't much to look at. In fact, it was a mess!

We hadn't received any mail since we left San Francisco and some of us stayed on the USS Dixie at night to sleep. Every morning the Mansfield boat picked us up and took us over to the Mansfield. We ate breakfast and lunch on the Mansfield and then went back to the Dixie for supper and for the rest of the night. We didn't have much work to do during the day because they had the Japanese doing most of it.

My brother Ray went to school at Albright College with a fellow by the name of Bob Harper. He was called back in the Navy about the time that I was and he evidently was assigned to the USS Dixie. He and 40 other fellows reported aboard. They came across the Pacific by ship instead of flying so it took them a little longer. I got a chance to talk to him and it sure felt good to talk to someone from Reading again.

On October 16 I was still aboard the Mansfield and the Dixie. We were waiting to see how many fellows would be transferred from the Mansfield before it went back to the States. We finally got paid for the first time since we left Philadelphia.

I received a letter from my mother but still hadn't received a letter from Betty since I got out there. It took my mother's letter eight days to arrive via airmail, so I guessed the mail was a little slow. My mother mentioned though that Bill Morris was called back into the Navy and that he had to report on October 16. I felt sorry for him!

That day a boat came along side of the Dixie to unload 56 survivors from two ships that had hit mines just like the Mansfield. Some of them were in pretty bad shape.

On October 17 I finally got three letters from Betty, another from my mother and one from my brother. That was great. According to Betty's letters it looked as if we were going to have a family! The doctor said the baby was due about June 4. I hoped I could get home by then.

I talked to a fellow who was a survivor from the minesweeper, Magpie. They hit a mine, and the ship sank, losing 21 men out of 37. One of the men was his best buddy. They were both from Philipsburg, NJ and he was the best man at his buddy's wedding in July, and his buddy's wife was pregnant. This fellow told me that he was regular Navy and had been in for 12 years. His buddy was a Reserve and had just been called back in the Navy.

He said to me, "Just let me hear anyone say anything bad about the Reserves after that." We Reservists had been taking a lot of teasing and abuse from some of the regular Navy fellows because they didn't like us Reserves very much. I guess they felt threatened that we might take their jobs. They could have them as far as we were concerned, we didn't want them anyway!

A couple of days prior I saw a new Reserve Naval officer coming aboard ship. When he came up the ladder I noticed that he had a camera hanging around his neck like a tourist and written across the front of his helmet was "Don't shoot, I'm a Reserve." On October 25 all of us fellows sleeping on the Dixie moved back to the Mansfield but it probably wasn't for very long. They transferred some fellows off the Mansfield, and that is why there was room for us, but I was afraid that they weren't finished with their transfers.

USS Jason

On October 26, at about 1100, another Sonarman and I were told to go up to the ship's office. They told us to pack and that we would be transferred in the afternoon. At 1600 we were transferred to Commander Service Division aboard the USS Jason. We were sent there for re-assignment and they said that we might get transferred from the Jason tomorrow.

Three days later I was notified that I was assigned to the USS Wallace L. Lind DD 703. I didn't know whether I had to sit around and wait until it came in or if I would eventually have to go chasing after it. Well, I ended up sitting, waiting around a few more days and had a chance to go ashore on liberty a few times. On one of the trips I even got to see Chief Petty Officer Merandy who used to be on the USS Loy when I was. I wasn't able to talk to him because I was just getting in the boat to go back to the ship when he was getting off. I did, however, have a chance to say hello and it was good to see him again.

USS Misspillion

At 0900 the morning of November 3 they told ten of us to pack our bags because we were getting transferred. At 0930 we were headed to the Navy tanker USS Misspillion AO 105 and were told that we would be taken to Korea where we would meet our assigned ships. The USS Misspillion was a fleet oiler that went out to refuel other ships at sea.

We left Sasebo at 1600 and headed our way to Wonsan, Korea. At that time we heard on the radio about the attempted assassination of President Truman.

Well, the trip to Wonsan took a little longer than the two expected days. We met up with a carrier and some destroyers and were busy refueling and delivering mail to the ships. We also delivered some of the ten fellows with me to their assigned ships.

On November 7, we finally got into Wonsan harbor and found out that the Lind wasn't there. I and a few other fellows were then transferred to the USS Hank DD 702 and as soon as we were on board the Hank, she left Wonsan. We proceeded all day to the north and finally that night, at about 2100, we met the USS Lind somewhere off of the northern coast of Korea and were transferred to it, bag and baggage, at sea, and in the dark of the night. What a dramatic entrance we made!

68

USS Wallace L. Lind

The Lind, built by the Federal Shipbuilding Corp. in Kearny, New Jersey, was rated as a 2200 ton (Short Hall) destroyer, and was commissioned in September 1944, in the New York Navy Yard. She was approximately 376 feet in length with a beam of 41 feet. It was twin screwed, steam turbine, geared,  driven with a total shaft horsepower of 60,000. The armament consisted of three 5"/38 twin mounts, 40MM and 20MM automatic machine guns, torpedo tubes as well as a depth charge battery.

She was named after Captain Wallace L. Lind, US Navy. Captain Lind died April 1940 and was awarded the Navy Cross for Distinguished Services as Executive Officer of the USS President Lincoln.

Well, after two months back in the Navy I finally found my ship and was onboard the Wallace L. Lind DD 703. They greeted us with coffee and sandwiches and seemed glad to see us. They were a little short of men and so far it seemed like a very nice ship with a friendly crew, much better than the Mansfield. The Captain and Commanding Officer of the Lind was Captain E. B. Carlson and The Executive Officer was Lieutenant Commander R. C. Marquardt.

After being on the Lind a couple days I came to the conclusion that the food was good and so was the company. Most of the fellows were from the area of Norfolk, Virginia and when we went back to the States we would probably go to Norfolk. Maybe I would get lucky and get transferred to the Lind after all.

On board I met a fellow from Reading, Pennsylvania by the name of Warren Mohn. He lived in the 1100 block of Locust Street and his wife was expecting to have their second child sometime that month. He was a Reserve who came back in the Navy September 8 through Philadelphia. It sure was nice to have someone to talk to about home.

We had been at sea most of the time since we arrived in Korea. For a few nights our job was to fire illuminating shells over the enemy lines to light up their position so our troops could better detect them.

From November 10 to 17 we did a lot of patrolling up and down the coast and once in a while we anchored in Wonsan harbor. Sometimes we fired on the enemy along the coastal highway as well as at the trains running along the tracks near the coast. One day we fired at a railroad tunnel after the train entered the tunnel and we were able to close both ends with our shell firing, trapping the train inside.

Every once in a while they sent us up to Chongjin in North Korea. When we got near there we had to go in through a narrow channel, past a buoy and then into a small harbor. We lay out in the harbor and fired various types of shells into the town to start fires and then we left. We did this every couple of days and the enemy must have noticed that we always passed near the buoy at the end of the channel.

So, while we were gone, they set up a six-inch gun in the mountains and zeroed it in on the buoy. The next time we came back, they were waiting for us, but we didn't come alone. That time an Australian destroyer came with us. We went into the channel first and right passed the buoy, and nothing happened; but, when the Australian destroyer passed the buoy the enemy fired and had two direct hits on the destroyer, killing a couple men. It didn't take long for both of our ships to zero in on the enemy gun and knock it out, but, I guess we learned a lesson, although this was the only entrance to the harbor.

On a lighter note, Mohn and I decided to grow mustaches. They were both coming along pretty good and we were seriously thinking about a beard also. As long as the Captain didn't say anything, we could.

On November 18 we went up to Sonjin and met the cruiser Rochester to pick up two passengers and then proceeded to Sasebo, Japan. The following night we got in to a real bad storm and our ship rolled and pitched every direction. I never got seasick before, but I sure did that night. I lost every bit of my supper. I wasn't ashamed because some of the fellows who had been on the ship three or four years even got sick. So, I guess it was pretty rough weather. We lost one boat, and some handrails were damaged. We finally reached Sasebo about 1500 and we expected to be there about one week. I really wanted to get my picture taken with my mustache! We were alongside the destroyer tender USS Dixie for about seven days of repairs.

On November 21 I went ashore to see Sasebo for a while and bought some presents. I also had my picture taken and bought a miniature camera. I didn't know if it was much good but at least I had the chance to take some pictures.

The next day I had the duty and my job was shore patrol at the Navy Anchor Club, which was the Navy beer hall in Sasebo. I was relieved at 1700 that evening without any trouble. Usually the fights started later in the evening after the fellows got drunk.

69

Thanksgiving: Nagasaki

November 23 was Thanksgiving and the day before they had a list on the board for those interested in going on a tour to Nagasaki. Mohn and I signed up and we were lucky enough to be picked. As you probably know, Nagasaki was one of the cities where we dropped the atom bomb. The tour cost $4.50. That included transportation, which was 85 miles each way from Sasebo to Nagasaki by bus, two big meals, the tour around the city by bus with a guide, and Coco-Cola to drink while riding on the bus. Even though it rained all day, we still had a very interesting and enjoyable trip. We left the ship at 0800 and arrived in Nagasaki about noon. We had dinner reserved for us at the Kanko, a new hotel in Nagasaki. We had some kind of fish for an appetizer and the most delicious steak that I have ever tasted for the main course.

We toured the city after dinner and stopped at the exact spot where the atom bomb was dropped. It was made into a little park as a memoriam of the event. We saw quite a bit of the damage that had been done, but most of the town had been rebuilt since. They built a museum on the exact location right where the bomb was dropped. It contained a lot of memorabilia such as bottles and a lot of other things that were half melted, showing how hot the heat from the bomb was. There were also a few clocks hanging on the wall that were stopped at the time of the explosion. Outside I saw a couple of concrete pillars and their shadows on the cement floor where the heat from the bomb had etched the cement floor darker every place but where the shadow was. I sure understood why so many people were killed here.

We then returned to the Kanko hotel for supper, which consisted of a very good lobster tail for an appetizer followed by a delicious turkey dinner. We ate like kings, left Nagasaki about 1900 and got back to our ship about 2300 that night. There were 25 of us who made this trip and we were sure glad we did.

Thanksgiving turned out to be an eventful day. Unfortunately, one of our big mail planes crashed on takeoff as it was leaving Sasebo. The other thing that happened was that we got 14 new men (all Reserves) aboard the Lind. Three of them were Sonarmen and two of those Sonarmen were from Pennsylvania. One was from Minersville

167

and worked at Parrish Pressed Steel in Reading. The other one was from Sellersville, up near Quakertown, and his father owned a hosiery mill which had a lot of Reading full fashioned knitting machines from Textile Machine Works. The name of the fellow from Sellersville was John Britch but I don't remember the name of the fellow from Minersville.

Pictured here: Willy Penman, Jack Linquest, Lewis Treat, Finerty and Charles Hayes (all Sonarmen).

November 24 was a red-letter day. The ship received 18 bags of mail and out of those 18 bags I received 10 letters!!! I got three from Betty, three from my mother, one from my brother, one from my uncle Will in California, one from Reverend Siegart, and one from Reverend Sharp. My brother's letter was all about a new friendship with a schoolteacher of the opposite sex and it sounded pretty serious.

On November 26 Mohn was notified that his wife gave birth to a little baby girl. He was really relieved because they both wanted a little girl. She was born on the 25th and the Fourth Naval District sent out a radio message to all ships in the fleet, eleven hours after it happened, that the baby was born. It was really great to celebrate with him. I found myself hoping that would happen to Betty and me one day.

Since we were in port, our mail seemed to be catching up to us a little better. Our ship got another seven bags of mail and of that I received three more letters. According to some of the letters, Betty was having a rough time with her pregnancy because of morning sickness. I was glad she was home with her parents instead of being alone. In one of her letters she talked about names for the baby and we had decided if it were a girl we would name her Marybeth, and if it were a boy we would name him Kenneth William. That same day we also heard on the radio that they were having a real big snowstorm on the east coast of the United States, especially around Philadelphia.

On November 28 we arrived back in Wonsan, Korea. We hit some rough weather on our journey but not as bad as when we went to Sasebo. Some of the fellows got seasick, but I didn't that time.

We were warned that we might have an air raid that night. We were a little anxious because that was one thing we hadn't had to worry about so far.

It had been much colder since we came back to Korea and the mountains along the coast were all covered with snow. It was cold for us but I imagined that it was much worse for the soldiers over on the land in all that freezing snow.

On November 30 we arrived in a northern Korea harbor off Hungnam. It was a good size town and we heard reports that 200,000 Chinese troops broke through our lines up north so we were expecting to get a little company. Upon our arrival, we relieved the USS Zellars, DD 777.

On December 1 we woke up and discovered our ship was all white,

covered with snow. It had snowed the night before and then got real cold so the snow and ice was pretty thick by morning. We had to shovel snow and chop the ice off the bulkheads and that was something new for me. I didn't remember having snow on the Loy like that! Although we did have some snow, we never had to shovel and chop. That evening they called for another storm and the mountains looked beautiful all covered in white. However, I imagined the poor devils on the beach fighting for their lives weren't appreciating it very much.

On December 3, Sunday morning they got a Protestant church group together and sent us over to the USS Mount McKinley AGC 7, which was a big communications ship. We had a nice church service and enjoyed ourselves very much.

One night I got a pleasant surprise while standing the mid-watch. Things were going pretty slow when I started to talk to the Officer of the Deck. We were both standing out in the bitter cold of the night, when he happened to mention that his home was in Atlanta, Georgia. Then I asked him if he was ever in Franklin, North Carolina and he said, "Hell yes!!" He said that was his old stomping grounds and I told him about Betty and me living there in Mrs. Leach's apartment. Then he asked me if I knew Betty Leach. It sure is a small world isn't it? He said he used to go to a Boy Scout camp in Mountain City down near Clayton. We talked about Franklin, Highlands, Clayton, Cherokee, and all those familiar places and before we knew it our mid-watch was over. It was a great night.

We then found out the Chinese communist troops were within 20 miles of Hungnam and were advancing. Our Marines were slowly retreating from up north and headed down into Hungnam. We moved in closer to the beach so that we could furnish as much fire support as possible in the event that they had to evacuate our troops.

For a while around December 12, we patrolled with the USS Massey maintaining the blockade on the northern patrol around Songjin. We traveled up and down the coast and did a lot of shore bombarding of targets that the shore spotters told us by radio to fire at. We were usually up half of the night firing at the enemy. We blew up a railroad bridge and some boxcars, fired on enemy concentrations and inspected sampans.

One piece of good news was that Mohn and I started to raise a beard to go along with our mustache.

On December 17, The USS Hank relieved us of our bombing duties and we headed back to Hungnam where we arrived later in the day. We were all happy to receive some mail when we arrived.

Back before I caught up with the Lind, and was floating around on the Mansfield, Dixie, and Misspillion, I wasn't getting my mail regularly, if at all. Evidently, Betty sent a letter of complaint to the Navy. With the mail that I received that day I received a letter from Commander Service Force, Pacific Fleet. The subject of the letter was mail delivery. They sent me a post card with it and instructed me to send it back to them to assist in a continuing mail handling time study. It took six weeks for me to get their letter; that ought to have told them something!

70

Hungnam evacuation

From December 18 to 22, we were very busy. Every day, at dusk, all ships were assigned several targets and instructed to fire upon them throughout the night. We anchored in as close as we could safely be and fired a couple shells every minute or so, just enough that the enemy was pinned down and couldn't move around. The Army and Marines had a perimeter set up around the town of Hungnam to protect those inside it as well as to keep out the enemy.

Every day, thousands of civilians were evacuated out of Hungnam, and the Marines that were retreating from the north were evacuated when they got there. In the meantime we held the perimeter to keep the enemy from getting the town. It was the Army's job to hold the perimeter during the day while we went out to sea and met an ammunitions ship. We then loaded ammunition all day, at sea, running side by side, in near zero temperatures and a lot of times in high winds.

Each day we got back to port in time to anchor and were assigned new targets and started firing at the enemy again for the whole night. If we didn't have the watch at night we tried to get some sleep and hoped that the gun they were firing wasn't over where we were sleeping. So, for about a week we didn't get much sleep. We were part of the United Nations naval vessels that were establishing a steel curtain around the shrinking defense perimeter encircling Hungnam. In coordination with the carrier-based air attacks, the pin point bombardment had made a no-man's land of the outer edges of the defense arc, as enemy concentrations, rear junctions, and vehicular traffic were

pounded day and night by us and other naval ships.

On December 23, we received the following message from the shore fire control party of the 3rd Infantry Division ashore, "The big wheels want to thank you guys for the swell job of naval gunfire in the past few days and hope you can keep it up. The boys on the front lines want to thank you, too."

By that time over 250,000 civilians were evacuated as well as most of the Marines and soldiers. Each day, as they evacuated, they moved the perimeter smaller and smaller, until they weren't holding much of the town anymore.

It was only a matter of time, and finally as dawn of December 24 broke cold and clear, and while most of the world began their holiday festivities, a relative quiet tenseness hung over the harbor and defense perimeter of Hungnam, Korea. It was D-Day. The remnant of troops, that for days had been methodically affecting their withdrawal into the small semicircle of protection within the harbor area, was evacuated.

The great armada of naval ships had been deployed about the harbor like so many chess men to cover the evacuating United States troops, and long before daylight, in the protection of darkness, all ships not participating in the evacuation had silently moved out of the harbor. The evacuation had been carefully planned and every ship had a specific function to perform, from the mighty battleship Missouri and the huge transport down to the small PF boats and LCMs. Early in the morning the small landing craft and amphibious boats began hovering about their mother ships making preparations to start for the beach to ship evacuations. Overhead carrier-based planes began making attacks on enemy concentrations; the air resounded with the boom of the big guns from the cruisers St. Paul and Rochester.

The Lind, Hank, Sperry, Massey, Zellars, and other destroyers lying in close to the beach kept up a continuous barrage of fire on strategic points.

At about 10 o'clock the landing craft started the final evacuation. LSTs beached and swallowed large quantities of men and equipment in true Higgins fashion. Tugs stood by to aid where needed. As transports loaded they moved out of the harbor.

Bryce Canon Destroyer Tender AD36
USS Wallace L Lind DD 703
USS Borie DD 704
USS Massey DD 778
USS Zellers DD 777

A little after noon, things really began in earnest. Between 1330 and 1630 the Lind fired 555 rounds of AAC, and that was really kicking them out. Empty brass shell cases littered the decks, fixtures blew loose from bulkheads, paint scales were everywhere, and tired handling crews kept passing ammunition as the Lind kept kicking them out.

At 1630 the demolition squads finished blowing up the dock facilities, and everything else that was of benefit to the enemy. Then it was time to leave, and one by one the ships fell in line and joined the long procession in the move south. Old Jolly  Wally with burned muzzles and littered decks was third from last to leave, and as she cleared the harbor Hungnam was nothing but a flaming mass of destruction.

Christmas Eve was a relief to everyone, knowing that the evacuation was over and that it was a success. We left Hungnam with the cruiser USS Rochester, and proceeded to Sasebo, Japan. The

Rochester sent us a message that we would not arrive in Sasebo until Tuesday morning, the day after Christmas. Then, our Captain sent a message to the Rochester, asking whether we couldn't possibly reach Sasebo by Christmas day. The Rochester sent back a message saying "There is a Santa Claus after all, we will arrive in Sasebo on Christmas day." So, we went full speed ahead and arrived in Sasebo late in the afternoon of Christmas day.

71

Christmas Day

We had Christmas dinner at sea and it was great! They put up a Christmas tree in the mess hall and while we were eating they played records of all the Christmas carols that we had.

We finally arrived in Sasebo about 1630 Christmas afternoon and that evening we got some mail. I was hoping to get some letters from Betty, but all I received was a Christmas card from Aunt Lillie and Aunt Ida. I did receive a package though from my mother and brother, containing juices, canned fruit, and a big can of pipe tobacco. That sure was timed right, getting the package on Christmas day.

It looked as if we would be staying in Sasebo for about a week. Evidently we needed quite a bit of repairs from the entire gun firing that we did. I guess we shook the ship apart. At least it gave our mail a chance to catch up to us. We were alongside the destroyer tender USS Jason for our repairs.

On December 28 we received lots of mail! That always helped to perk us up a little bit. I received five letters from Betty and a lot of Christmas cards from many of my friends. I had one surprise; I received a check for $51 from Textile Machine Works. It was my Christmas pay and boy was I surprised. I also received a Christmas card from a Mrs. George Post, who was a member of the Lima Methodist church. She wrote a nice note on the back of the card, and she mentioned that her son was lying in a soldier's grave somewhere in South Korea, having been killed in action on September 7.

Since they just called this a "police action" and not a war, it seemed as if it was just business as usual at home. Most people seemed to forget us

fellows over there and didn't realize there was a war going on unless they personally lost someone in the service or had a loved one over there.

I wanted to get home soon because my brother mentioned in his letter that he wanted me to be best man at his wedding. His relationship was getting pretty serious.

On December 28 Mohn and I went ashore and had our pictures taken together and they turned out pretty good. Both of us had beards and they were coming along.

We left Sasebo with the Hank and were on our way back to Korea headed toward the 38th parallel south of Wonsan to help support the Republic of Korea ROK division.

72

New Year's Eve

I spent New Year's Eve standing watch while we were on patrol. It was Navy custom that the Officer of the Deck, who had the mid-watch starting at midnight on New Year's Eve, had to write everything in his logbook in rhyme like a poem. Well, they printed in our "plan of the day" which they printed every morning, a copy of what the Officer of the Deck of the USS Hank wrote in his log. The Hank is the DD 702 and it operated with us. I think he wrote a pretty good poem and I would like to share it with you. Here it is:

Off the east Korean coast,
near the town of Chumongin,
the Happy Hank is steaming with the "Jolly Wally"
(W.L. Lind).
Outside the hundred fathom curve
where we're bound to stay,
it's a lot safer than inside where minefields lay,

The formation course is one-four-five true.
Steering three-two-five half the time, too.
Patrolling the coast back and forth
Two hours south and two hours north.

At a speed of five knots, which really isn't much,
for this high speed destroyer wasn't built for such.
A slow speed, but the slower we go,
the longer we stay out of old Sasebo.

The Hank is guide and OTC,
steaming split plant on boilers one and three.
The Lind is astern one thousand yards hence,
aiding our efforts of coastal defense.

By keeping a blockade as tight as can be,
letting nothing approach the land from the sea.
In addition to blockading an additional chore,

is standing by to support the first ROK Corps.

The ship is in readiness condition three,
and also darkened making it tough to see.
Material condition Baker is set,
all equipment is operating the best it has yet.

Standing by nearby in Mine Division One,
to continue sweeping with the morning sun.
The Captains in the sea cabin,
The Exec is down below.

When, this cold mid-watch is over,
that's where I'm going to be.

Isn't that a great poem?

On January 1, 1951 we had our New Year's dinner while patrolling somewhere off Korea near the 38th parallel. We did a lot of patrolling with other ships in our division since we got back to Korea. Our objective was to form a blockade to keep the enemy from going in or out and also to conduct shore bombardments. Another destroyer in our division, the USS Sperry, went in a little too close to shore and was fired upon from shore batteries and was hit by three shells. Fortunately, only one fellow was hurt, and it wasn't serious.

January 7 was an interesting day. First of all we were up most of the night doing a lot of firing at the enemy. The next morning one of our minesweepers went in too close to the beach and ran aground. Later that day our Destroyer Division Commodore fell over the side of his flagship and they had to put a boat in the water to pick him up. On top of all of that it snowed steadily. The only good thing was that the DD 704 dropped us some mail. I received 10 letters and three cards!

January 8 we were up most of the night firing on enemy troops that were ashore. The following day we stood by to help a burning Siamese corvette. The weather was rough and we had a lot of snow as well. During the night we bombarded the enemy with harassing fire.

By January 13, the weather finally cleared and we helped to sink the Siamese Corvette "Prosae" which had been burning for several days. I guess they decided that it was too damaged to try to save. We fired 5" 38 caliber shells at it and watched it explode.

Here is another poem written by one of the shipmates:

179

(With apologies to the author of the Old Sea Chantey-by an Old Salt Anonymous.)

> The Lind was firing on the Prosae
> And she blew, she blew.
> The Lind was firing on the Prosae
> And she blew, she blew.
> She exploded from a five inch hit
> And she blew, blew, blew, blew.
> And shook the Korean coast
> Oh mister how she blew.

The movie shown that evening was "Sea Hawk" with Errol Flynn and Brenda Marhall. It was 3 reels and 104 minutes long.

From January 14 to January 19 we proceeded down the coast to Bakuko to give the Army fire support and to relieve the USS Hank. We anchored offshore and gave the fire support for five days.

At 0730 on January 20 the USS English and the USS Massey arrived in the area for a conference. Soon after the conference we started on our way back to Sasebo after spending three weeks off the coast of Korea. We expected to arrive the next morning. The ship received a commendatory message from Commander Task Force 95, Admiral Smith, for the intelligence and communication work we had done during the past week.

We also received a message from the Commander Naval Forces, received from Prince Pisit Diskul Commanding General Thai Expeditionary Forces with the United Nations Command:

> *"As Chief of the Thai Military Liaison and Commanding General of the Thai Expeditionary Forces with the United Nations Command, permit me to place on record the deepest appreciation of his Thai Majesty's Government as well as of his Majesty's Armed Forces for the gallant and successful rescue operation of the men of his Majesty's corvette Prosae which was recently aground at Kis-amun-Dan off the eastern Korean coast during an active engagement with the enemy ashore.*
>
> *"On behalf of his Majesty's Armed Forces and of the Royal Navy in particular I beg of your*

Admiral to convey to your command as well as to the commanding officers and men of the ships concerned who took part in the rescue operation and in the ensuing brave attempt to refloat the Prosae in expression of our most grateful thanks for all that they did to help their Brave Comrades in arms."

"The Thai people of all ranks and files have been overwhelmingly touched by and are profoundly appreciative of this action on the part of the officers and men in question which exemplifies not only the spirit of comradeship but also the cordial friendship between our two peoples which I am sure will go into the annul of the present struggle for the ideals of the United Nations with which we are bound in solidarity. Desire that the Substance of this letter be made known, to all concerned."

We all felt pretty good about hearing this news! When we left Sasebo, the Captain ordered everyone to stop shaving because we were going to have a beard growing contest and anyone caught shaving would be restricted in the next liberty port. Anyone with a beard at the start of the contest automatically became a judge, which included me. The day before we returned to Sasebo, we ended the contest and a dozen of us went around inspecting all the beards. The ship gave a prize to the man with the best beard and a booby prize for the tender one who had the least fuzz on his face. First prize went to a 62 year old man with a white beard who received a beautiful pair of red plaid Scottish shorts. The booby prize went to a young fellow who had never shaved. He received a miniature Donald Duck.

According to Betty's last letter, Junior was beginning to make himself or herself known. Betty was beginning to feel much better with her pregnancy. She had to stay in bed quite a bit of the time in the beginning.

Now the bad news; the Captain announced that everyone had to shave off the beards and mustaches. That meant me too. I was pretty disappointed because mine was just beginning to look good. I had a lot of compliments on it and it was a pretty shade of red. But the Captain said shave so who was I to argue?

We arrived in Sasebo about noon on Sunday January 21 with everyone clean-shaven. We expected to stay about a week because there were more repairs to be made to the ship and a lot of supplies to be loaded. We tied up alongside the destroyer tender USS Hector AD 7. Before we left port again, I managed to send a telegram to Betty and also get a package sent home.

On January 27 I found out that my Reserve enlistment would run out on March 18 and then they would tack on "Harry's year." At the start of the Korean Conflict President Harry Truman passed a ruling that if your Reserve time ran out right now he added one year to it. This is what happened to me.

The following day I went ashore with a recreation party. They sent 75 men from the Lind and 75 men from the USS Thompson (DMS38). They had free beer and sandwiches for us that tasted pretty good. The party started early in the afternoon and the fellows played baseball, football and ping pong. I enjoyed playing football and ping pong. Later that afternoon four fellows from the Lind challenged four of our fellows to a boxing match. Our ship lost three out of the four matches. After the boxing matches they had a show for us, which featured Japanese entertainers. It consisted of a band, some dancers and a magician. They all were very talented and entertaining. After the show our basketball team challenged the Thompson team and lost 54 to 37. We all had a good time and arrived back on our ship by 2200.

Around 0830, January 29, we left Sasebo and proceeded to Korea with the tanker USS Cimaron. By midnight we met a large invasion force off of the East coast of Korea including the battleship Missouri, the cruiser Manchester, the destroyer tender Dixie, and many other destroyers. We bombarded the beach somewhere around the 37th Parallel near Konsong.

73

ROK Agents Spies

On February 1 we were sent to Bokuko, Korea to pick up 15 Korean intelligence agents and two American agents. Two or three of the men were officers and they were assigned bunks in the officers' quarters. The rest were enlisted men so they were assigned bunks in our department. When they came aboard we noticed that they were pretty dirty and it didn't take too long to tell that they didn't smell too good either. Some of the fellows got after them about taking baths. They could speak some English and refused to take a bath because if they went ashore smelling like a rose, they would stick out like a sore thumb and would soon be discovered as spies. So, we just had to put up with the bad smell.

On February 2 we proceeded to Wonsan. We were supposed to drop off the ROK agents but the weather was too rough for a boat. The following day we were sent to pick up survivors of the sunken AMS Partlage that hit a mine. It turned out that we weren't needed so we proceeded to Chongjin to drop off our intelligence party.

On the morning of February 4 we dropped off the ROK agents. Then we proceeded south, bombarding the coast as we went. The man in charge of the intelligence party was a Republic Of Korea Major. He stayed aboard our ship so he could communicate to the agents by radio. We were supposed to come back at a pre-arranged time and establish contact with the agents. If they had any information to give to us that was the way we got it and then passed it on to headquarters.

On February 5 we returned to the place where we had dropped them off and tried to establish radio contact. After a while someone answered, saying it was the ROK agents, but right away the Major knew there was something wrong. He told us that it wasn't them and that they were being impersonated. We continued to talk to them and they said they were all right but they needed money, food, and guns. We told them we had to go to Pusan to get everything and that we would be back in two nights.

After a fast trip to Pusan we arrived back to our previous location off the coast of Korea where we had dropped off our agents. It was dark and we soon re-established radio contact with the men on the shore. After talking to them for a while, the Major still insisted that they were not his agents even though they claimed to be. They asked whether we brought them food, money and guns. We told them that we did and that we would start bringing everything in to them by boat. Because it was dark, they couldn't see us out at sea so we slowly moved the ship in a little closer to shore.

We had two of our fellows communicating with walkie-talkies to each other, even though they were still on the ship. If the enemy were listening over the radio, it sounded to them as if we were sending in a boat. The fellow on walkie-talkie #1 said, "We have the boat in the water now and we are on our way in toward the beach." Walkie-talkie #2 replied, "Let us know when you can see the beach." In the meantime, we called the people on the beach and told them that a boat was on the way with the supplies they requested. We waited for a reasonable length of time and then walkie-talkie #1 said, "We are about half way in to the beach but because of extremely high swells we are having difficulty in seeing the beach." Then walkie-talkie #2 responded, "Roger. We will see what we can do."

Then our ship called the people on the beach and explained that our boat was having trouble seeing the beach due to the weather. We asked them if they could have as many people as possible come down on the beach to help unload the boat. We asked if they could shine a light straight up into the air to help the boat find them. They called back and said that they would do that. By that time our ship had eased in closer to shore, and pretty soon we were able to see the light shining into the air.

All of our guns were trained on this position and soon we opened fire on them. Our Major said that they then started to swear at us in Korean and then suddenly the radio went quiet. I don't know whether we ever found out any more about how many people we might have killed that night but we did find out that three of our agents had been killed. The rest were all right and a little farther north. The Major was right; those men were imposters.

During the same time we worked with the ROK agents, we also operated with some of the other ships in our division. They were the destroyers English, Zellars, Borie, and Ozbourn. The English was our division flagship and we were Division 161. Although we didn't always sail together, there were quite a few ships in our division including the Lind, the Massey, the Sperry and the Hank.

As usual, we did a lot of shore bombarding and we patrolled the coast from the north and south of Wonsan harbor. We had to ensure that the enemy didn't get in or out. Unfortunately, shore batteries sank a minesweeper that was working with us. The communists claimed they sank two destroyers but in truth it was one minesweeper and they hit the destroyer Ozburn. The damage was very slight. We spent a lot of time looking for survivors from the minesweeper, but didn't find any.

After we lost our three agents, we picked up more of them at Pusan and dropped them off behind the lines. We continued our other duties with ships in our division and I believe we were the only ship that was working with the agents. I know that it was very top secret. We weren't allowed to talk about it to anyone and especially not write home about it. One time the Captain said that although we would never read in the newspapers about what we were doing on those secret missions, some day we could tell our grandchildren about it.

On February 6 we proceeded north to Chongjin to talk to our intelligence men on the beach. Then we did some shore bombarding. Two days later we bombarded the beach around Kongsong and then later we proceeded to Pohang where we dropped off some intelligence men. After we headed to Wonsan for a brief time, we rendezvoused with the HMAS Warramunga and proceeded to Chongjin, Korea. At 2000 we established communication with the Chongjin intelligence team. Upon completion we proceeded to Pusan.

On February 12 we arrived in Pusan at about 0800. While the Captain and some of our officers were ashore at a meeting, we went ashore and had a beer party. We got underway for Wonsan at 2200.

On February 13, at 0500, we rendezvoused with the USS English above the 38th parallel. We dropped off an intelligence party at 2000 just a few miles south of Wonsan. On Valentine's Day we spent the day patrolling and furnishing fire support for troops above the 38th parallel. The following day we were off the coast of Korea and north of the enemy lines. The Major directed us to a point where he thought there were some enemy troops. A little later we got close enough to shore to see some buildings and some people near the beach. We could see there were some soldiers, but it also looked as if there might be women and children. The Major ordered the Captain to fire on them and the Captain said, "There are women and children!" The Major replied, "Little communists, big communists, fire!" And we fired. I don't know how many we killed but it was too many.

We then proceeded to Chongjin with the USS Ozbourn and we put an intelligence team ashore and then we bombarded the railroad that ran along the coast. We also bombarded a small village.

74

Wonsan Bombardment

On February 16 we proceeded to Wonsan and anchored in the inner harbor about 1700. We bombarded targets all night and we began a concentrated bombardment of the Wonsan along with many United Nation ships. The effort was designed to disrupt communist traffic through the key city on the east coast supply and reinforcement route from Manchuria. Ships involved included our sister ship the English, the battleship Missouri and many ships from other nations. Navy marksmanship proved itself as our destroyers hit moving locomotives from a range of several miles while pitching and rolling in the heavy seas.

The morning of the 17th, we left for Chongjin where we established contact with the intelligence team. We bombarded the town the rest of the evening. The day after, we refueled and re-armed at sea. We then proceeded to Wonsan so that we could send in supplies to the intelligence teams.

By the 20th we had bombarded inner Wonsan harbor and established contact with the intelligence team and sent in the supplies. We also picked up the pilot of a Corsair that was shot down in enemy waters. He was all right except for being half frozen. The Lind, Ozbourn and Sperry were all shot at by shore batteries. It didn't take long to silence the batteries with our guns.

On February 21 we bombarded shore batteries until 1200. We then proceeded to buoy #4 to communicate with the shore intelligence party. The next day we got underway to meet the replenishment group.

We refueled at sea from a tanker and then transferred our pilot back to the aircraft carrier Valley Forge. We then proceeded to Pusan.

By February 23 we fired our 6,000th five inch shell since being in Korea. For each shell there was also a big powder case to handle. That was quite a bit of shooting and ammunition handling!

On the 24th of February we pulled into Pusan for supplies and then met up with the hospital ship Consolation. This was the same ship that was in Hungnam. They sent me over to it again, and I got the same dentist that I had when I went to the dentist in Hungnam. He filled two teeth, and he told me that I'd better soon have one of my molars pulled, before it gave me trouble. We left Pusan again by midnight and headed back for Wonsan with more ROK intelligence men.

From February 25 to 27 we spent our time in the inner harbor of Wonsan for shore bombarding during the day and at night we anchored near buoy #4 to communicate with our intelligence team on the beach. We left on the 28th and proceeded north about 50 miles to do some shore bombarding and then dropped off our intelligence team. We then proceeded back to the inner harbor of Wonsan for more shore bombardment until dark and then back out to buoy #4.

On March 1 the Captain made one of his famous speeches. We were originally scheduled to go in the Navy yard on the east coast about May 1st, but they decided they needed us out there longer than they had originally expected. So we were scheduled for the Navy yard about June 14th. That sure was disappointing. The next day the weather started to turn real cold and the sea was getting pretty rough and uncomfortable.

By nightfall the temperature was down around zero. We got orders to go to Pusan for supplies and on the morning of March 3 we arrived in Pusan all covered with ice. Because of the bad weather the night before and with the waves coming up over the ship, we looked like an icicle the next morning. We had to do a lot of ice chopping and we were happy to receive some mail when we arrived. I got 3 letters from Raymond. He said that he was going to give Eva an engagement ring but he didn't mention anything about when the wedding would be. I hoped he was going to wait until I got home.

March 4 was Sunday holiday routine. We stayed overnight and then we were on our way back to Wonsan for more blockade patrolling and bombarding. At about 1700 we rendezvoused with the Borie and received a large quantity of mail aboard. That made everyone happy!

The following newspaper clipping is quoted for interest. Mrs. Lind christened this ship:

"Mrs. Wallace L. Lind, 60, widow of a naval captain, died here yesterday after a long illness. In recent years she lived with a son, Wallace L. Lind, Jr., at 2238 North Burlington Street, Arlington. Mrs. Lind, the former Hazel Bagley, was born in Wellsville, Missouri. She attended finishing schools in New York City and in Europe. Having lived here most of the time since 1935, she and Captain Lind resided for a number of years at the Kennedy Warren Apartments. Captain Lind, holder of the Navy Cross and former Commander of the Battleship Omaha, collapsed and died in 1940 on a Baltimore pier shortly after greeting his son who had just disembarked from a ship from the West Indies. Mrs. Lind has been active here in the Red Cross and was on the board of the Soldiers, Sailors, and Marines Club.

Her only immediate survivor is her son, who is management adviser in the office of the Assistant Chief of Naval Personnel. Graveside services will be held at 2 P.M. tomorrow at Arlington Cemetery."

The Captain sent the following letter to Mrs. Lind's son:

"Dear Mr. Lind,

It is with regret that we learned of the death of your mother, Mrs. Wallace L. Lind. The officers and crew of the USS Wallace L. Lind join me in extending our deepest sympathy to you and your family.

We are very proud of our ship named after your father. It may interest you to know that we have been blockading and bombarding the East Coast of Korea since early October and in that time have fired over six thousand rounds of five inch ammunition.

Sincerely Yours,

E.B. Carlson,
Commander, U.S. Navy Commanding
R.C. Marquardt,
LCDR U.S. Navy
Executive Officer"

On March 5 we arrived back at Wonsan and went into the inner harbor at 0700 to give the USS English 600 rounds of ammunition. At 1300 we proceeded back out to buoy #4. On March 6 we met the replenishing group at 1000 to refuel and take on more ammo. At 1500 we proceeded to Chonqjin to drop off another intelligence team. At 2400 we left to go to Songjin.

On March 9 early Saturday morning we received orders to go to Pusan. We arrived there at about 1730, but were not able to leave the ship and by midnight we were on our way back to Wonsan. We were told that no one was allowed to go ashore because there was an epidemic of Bubonic Plaque plus and an outbreak of Typhus and Smallpox.

We were placed under quarantine and we weren't allowed to enter any port for at least a week. They claimed that someone had been aboard our ship recently that had been exposed to the Bubonic Plaque and then soon after leaving our ship died from it. So, we all got inoculated for Bubonic Plaque and waited another seven days for the next inoculation.

On Sunday, March 11 the weather calmed and was much warmer. They set "Holiday Routine" because it was Sunday and that meant we didn't have to work other than standing normal watch. Of course, it hardly ever worked out that way because there were always unexpected projects that came up. I guess they had us do all that work on Sundays so that it didn't interfere with our bombarding the beach all week. At 0815 we met the replenishment ship and were told that we would follow the USS Walke in getting fuel and ammo. At 1700 we proceeded to buoy #4 to establish radio communications with the party ashore.

The cruiser USS Manchester had been with us quite a bit. On Wednesday March 14th we fired our 7,000th five inch shell.

On March 15th Betty sent the following from a newspaper clipping from back home:

Nothing Moves

"Nothing moves in Wonsan without our knowledge. It is a city of death," one high-ranking U. S. Naval officer said. The biggest day's score for the UN surface force was chalked up March 15th at 11am. Then the light cruiser Manchester, destroyers English and Eversten and the patrol frigates Burlington, Glendale and Sausalito opened up

189

simultaneously on a troop billeting area. Five minutes later the gunfire ceased and aerial photoreconnaissance planes scouted the area. The photographs revealed 6,000 enemy casualties. At 1pm the destroyer Wallace L. Lind opened fire on another barracks. Two minutes later, all that remained were ruins and 2,000 dead or wounded soldiers."

On Saturday, March 17 we were supposed to be relieved by the USS Zellars on Thursday night and then leave for Sasebo at 0700 Friday morning. Well, the Zellars didn't relieve us until Friday afternoon and we bombarded Wonsan all day Friday. After the Zellars finally relieved us, we started for Sasebo about 1800. As we were leaving Wonsan harbor, the enemy shore batteries fired at us and just about every other ship in the harbor. All the ships fired back as fast as they could until we had knocked out all of the shore batteries.

Only one of our ships got hit (not the Lind), but most of us had some close ones. After all this happened they decided to keep us in Wonsan for a little while longer. On Friday afternoon we fired our 8,000th five inch shell and by that evening we were close to our 9,000th five inch shell fired. We fired our guns so much that the gun barrels got very hot and burned all of the paint off of the barrels. That's a lot of firing! I'm glad that I wasn't on the other end of those barrels.

75

Repairs in Sasebo

We arrived in Sasebo on March 17 and stayed for one week to make repairs alongside a destroyer tender. We hoped we would be in Sasebo over Easter. When the Zellars relieved us, they dropped off some mail for us and I received about seven letters. Oh yes, I almost forgot, we also received our second inoculation. We hoped that took care of the problem.

As we were getting relieved, the following two messages were exchanged between the cruiser Manchester and the Lind

"From: USS W.L. Lind
To: USS Manchester

'Captain good morning. Every time they let us shoot we stir them up so they shoot back. Signed Carlson.'

From: USS Manchester
To: USS W.L. Lind

'Let sleeping dogs and commies sleep so I can get some too. Top of the morning to you. Your operations and accomplishments in past month have been outstanding. Pleasant period of relaxation to good ship Lind. Signed Rear Admiral Allan E. Smith.'"

On Palm Sunday, March 18, we arrived in Sasebo about 1230 and tied up alongside the repair ship USS Jason ARH-1. We stayed there for the whole week for repairs and to get supplies and a little recreation before we headed back to Wonsan.

On Monday March 26 we got underway at 0630 for Pusan. A plane came out to meet us and we fired at a sleeve about 1230. We arrived in Pusan at 1730 and at 2200 we were on our way to Wonsan.

On March 27 we arrived in Wonsan in the morning and refueled at 1230. We got underway again at 1800 for Songjin and arrived there about 2400. We spent the last four days around Songjin and Chongjin firing on bridges and railroad yards and a lot of road junctions. When we weren't firing our guns, we were running out someplace to meet a replenishing group to refuel and take on more ammunition.

On April 5 we returned to Sonjin at 0600 and went to a position south of Sonajin for pre-D-Day bombardment and also to cover some minesweepers. We fired all day and all night in company with the cruiser St. Paul and the destroyer Massey.

On D-Day, April 7, we started bombarding at 0600. At 0800 the Royal Marines went ashore on a commando raid. We searched all evening for a downed pilot but never found him. Then we left for Sasebo for emergency repairs.

On April 9 we were underway to Sasebo and entered Sasebo about 1200. We went alongside the USS Prairie at 1330 for repairs from April 11 to 18. After leaving Sasebo we spent our time between Wonsan, Songjin, and Chongjin. During that time we did a lot of shore bombarding, meeting replenishing ships to refuel, took on more ammunition and went back in to do more firing. We did that until the 18th, and were relieved at Songjin at 2000 and we proceeded to rendezvous with the aircraft carrier USS Boxer.

On April 19 we met the replenishing group and refueled at 0700. We started for Yokosuka at 2000 with the USS Boxer, Borie, Massey, and Zellars at the speed of 25 knots.

On April 21 we arrived in Yokosuka at 1200 and tied up alongside the USS Bryce Canyon.

We had spent the next nine days in Yokosuka cleaning up the ship and taking on supplies. At 0530 on April 30 we got underway with all of our division. We were Division 161. Also with us was the USS Boxer and we proceeded to the combat area at 25 knots.

Early morning on May 2, we rendezvoused with a replenishing group and refueled at 0530. Later we rendezvoused with Task Force 77, which included the aircraft carriers Boxer, Princetown, Philippine Sea, 12 destroyers plus the cruisers Helena, Manchester, and Belfast.

On May 8 after cruising with Task Force 77 for almost a week, we refueled from a tanker in a nearby replenishment group.

On May 9 our Division 161was relieved by Division 131 at 1300 and we proceeded to Yokosuka. We arrived there at 0900 on May 11 and spent the day off loading ammunition and then got underway at 2400. We were headed for home and our first stop was

Midway! We arrived there at 0700 and had a brief party before we headed back to sea by 1030.

By 0800, on May 18 we made a full power run, making 32 knots until 1600.

We arrived in Pearl Harbor at 0930 on May 19, Armed Forces Day. We were beginning to get a little excited. It was hard to believe, but it was gradually sinking in that we would be home soon!

We got underway at 0620 on May 21...San Diego, California here we come!!

Even though we were well on our way home, the bombarding of Wonsan continued. This clipping was taken from a newspaper back home and sent to me by Betty. Date lined May 22: "Sixteen inch shells from the US battleship New Jersey carried the unprecedented naval bombardment of Wonsan on Korea's east coast into its 96th straight day today. The Far East Fleet flagship joined the siege of Wonsan yesterday. Its arrival brought to 50 the number of battleships, cruisers, destroyers, patrol frigates and minesweepers from six different countries that have taken part in the non-stop bombardment. The New Jersey's one ton shells were the first of that size to hit Wonsan since its sister ship, the USS Missouri, bombarded the port city March 1."

At 0730, May 26, we arrived in San Diego and tied up at the Broadway Pier. Since it was rather special arriving in San Diego everyone decided, on the way from Pearl Harbor, that we would have an "anchor pool." There were 60 envelopes. Each had a number in it from 1 to 60. Each envelope was sold for $10, which made the total $600.00. The idea was that when we arrived in San Diego and anchored or tied up at a dock or tied up alongside another ship, whichever it would be, the official time was written in the ship's log.

Once we knew the official time we then knew what minute was the winner. The 60 numbers in the envelopes stood for the minutes of the hour. Ducky Mohn and I each invested the $10.00 in an envelope and would you believe it, Mohn won! That was a nice coming home present for him. We were soon allowed off of the ship. Many of the fellows had wives and families waiting on the dock for them. By 1100 I made it to a telephone and called Betty. It was nice talking to her and knowing that I was back in the United States and that much closer to home. We were so happy because it wouldn't be long until our baby was born.

Those fellows who were lucky enough to have their families meet them at the dock were able to get off of the ship until we left again. The rest of us got liberty for our brief stay in San Diego.

193

We got underway at 0630 on May 28 and headed for Panama. We did a lot of chipping paint and painting. It was business as usual...I guess they wanted us to look good when we returned home. We didn't paint much outside because we were approaching a hurricane and it was getting rough and wet.

76

Balboa, Panama

Our baby was due on June 4! Fortunately we were able to go around most of the hurricane so the weather wasn't too bad. We arrived in Panama at 0700. They announced that we would have liberty late afternoon but that we would be painting most of the day. They put the deck force over the side to paint the sides of the ship. Since I was in the O division we were responsible for painting the bridge and the mast. Guess who got the job painting the top part of the mast? I got the job painting the cross member of the mast 90 feet in the air!

I climbed up with a bucket of paint and shinned out to the end of the cross member and painted my way back. While I was up there the deck force was over the side painting, the gun crews were cleaning their guns right beneath me, and the engineers were refueling the ship. Also, the signalmen were putting their freshly laundered flags back into their flag bags, which were situated right under where I was painting. When I ran out of paint and I had to lower my paint can on a line to have it refilled.

As I was pulling the filled paint can up the line, the can slipped out of the sling, tumbled down and sprayed paint all over the freshly cleaned guns and ended up in the flag bag of freshly laundered flags. Well you can imagine I wasn't too popular at that particular moment. In fact, if I wasn't up so high, I think some of them might have come up after me. It didn't take me very long to decide that I'd better stay up on the mast for a while!

Fortunately for me, something else happened at the same time that I dropped the paint. As I said before, the engineers were refueling the ship and the deck force was over the side painting the sides of the ship right down to the water line. To refuel the ship they had to bring a four inch hose from the dock over to the ship and insert it into the trunk where they put the fuel hose. Then they pumped oil into the fuel tanks under various crew compartments and also under some of the main deck. The engineers opened various vent caps so that they could see down into the fuel tanks and tell when the tanks were near full.

They were supposed to have someone stationed at each of the open vents and evidently that didn't happen that day. Just as I dropped the can of paint, oil started spilling out of one of the vents onto the main deck and no one noticed the oil running all over the deck and down the freshly painted side. Most of the deck force had just completed painting the side of the ship and were putting away the slings that they had over the side to stand on while they were painting.

They also were about ready to take a shower so that they could go ashore on a well-deserved liberty. Then all hell broke loose. The oil kept coming until someone noticed it running all over the deck. Eventually someone yelled to shut off the oil but by then the fresh paint job was covered in oil! When all this excitement happened, everyone who had been glaring up at me turned their attention to the oil slick.

It didn't take me long to figure out that this was my big chance and I was down the mast and out of there before anyone knew what happened.

Pretty soon we heard an announcement over the PA system that there would be no liberty until the oil was cleaned up and the side was repainted. Well, that almost caused a mutiny. Most of the fellows that had started to clean up and get ready for liberty continued to do so. It took a while, but eventually they made the announcement that the liberty party could leave the ship immediately, unless they were in the engineering department. The whole engineering department had to stay aboard ship, clean up the mess and repaint the side of the ship.

I happened to be scheduled for liberty, and you can believe it, that anyone who had liberty got off of that ship as fast as they could! We never knew when they might change their mind and make everyone clean up the mess. It's funny because after all of that, everyone seemed to forget about the fellow that was painting the mast.

On the morning of June 5, the ship looked spic and span and at 0800 we started through the Panama Canal. It took us until 1630 to get through and by 1900 we were underway and on our way to Norfolk.

Welcome Marybeth and home at last! Ever since we left the canal I had been anxiously wondering if I was a father yet. At 2000 my wondering was over. I received a radiogram from the radio shack telling me that Marybeth Fidler was born at 0753 that morning. I was so relieved to know that everything was all right and that we had a little girl! I didn't find out until later that the Navy wouldn't allow them to send me a personal message announcing the baby, but that Reverend Sharp contacted a friend in the Navy department and he took care of it. So, what they did was send a message to all ships in the

Atlantic fleet that Marybeth, the daughter of Kenneth H. Fidler of the Wallace L. Lind, was born. Our ship copied the message and gave it to me! I earlier mentioned that this is the way Mohn was notified.

By June 8, we were closer to home and we were told that an airplane would soon be flying overhead and that we were supposed to drop a full pattern of depth charges while they took photographs. It was supposed to be some sort of a structural test to see how the ship held up, or I guess, more like how the ship held together.

On June 9 we arrived home at last!! We pulled into Norfolk at 1000 and tied up at the Convoy Escort pier. The crew had already been told which half of the crew would be getting leave first and, of course, I had made sure that I was in that group. All of us in the first leave party, and those who had liberty the first night, were ready to leave the ship as soon as they passed the word. A few minutes later the announcement came and we were out of there!

Ducky Mohn and I decided the quickest way home was to get out to the main road and hitchhike. So that is what we did and we were very fortunate to get a ride almost right away. Two other sailors picked us up and they were on the way to their home in New York State. They went right through Chester, where Betty was and I believe Ducky had to hitch another ride from there to Reading where he lived.

Around 2000 I was in the Chester hospital to see Betty after not seeing her for almost nine months. Also, I got my first look at the best of the family, our daughter, Marybeth. She really looked great and it felt so good to be home together as a family.

The next 30 days went so fast I hardly remembered what happened. Soon after I arrived home, Betty and Marybeth were released from the hospital and we spent most of the time at Betty's parents' house in Chester. I don't remember just how soon I was able go home to Reading to see my mother. I don't even remember if I went home alone or if Betty and the baby were able to travel with me. As soon as I got off the ship and started for Chester I am sorry to say I stopped writing in my diary. So, from here on I'll have to wing it. I think most of the 30 days that I was home on leave, it took a little time to get adjusted to being home again and having a baby in the family. I'm sure we made visits to Reading and also around Philadelphia to show off our baby to our friends.

It wasn't long until the 30 days leave was over and I had to go back to the ship. That part was hard but you have to remember that half of the crew didn't get their leave and were anxiously waiting for us to return to the ship so that they could go home. Some of them who didn't live too far away were able to go home on liberty, or weekend pass these first 30 days but there were some that lived a great distance that were still waiting to return home.

When Ducky and I returned to the ship I took my car along and parked it at the ferry terminal and we took the ferry over to Norfolk. It didn't take us very long to figure out that we could switch our watches, and duty time, around so that we would be free to go home on weekends. This worked out pretty good because there was usually someone willing to trade watches or duty so that they could get ashore during the week. We had to stay aboard some weekends but not too many.

I think Ducky usually came along to Chester with me and then hitched a ride to Reading. I still remember one weekend that he came along home and then he was supposed to meet me in Chester Sunday night about 2200. We were going to drive all night and get down in time to take the last ferry to Norfolk and be on the ship by 0800. Right before we left our house in Chester, Betty's mother gave us a bag of fruit to take along to eat on the way back. We did eat some of it but we had some left and when we arrived at the ferry we just had time to park the car and run to catch the ferry and, of course, we forgot to take the bag of fruit with us.

It was hot that week and when we arrived back at the car the following Friday to start back to Chester - wow! I opened the car door and there must have been a million fruit flies in there as well as a bag of rotten fruit on the front seat. We threw out the fruit and started home to Chester, fruit flies and all. We put the windows down and as long as we were moving the flies were in the back seat but every time I had to stop for a traffic light, they swarmed around our heads! By the time we arrived in Chester, we still had at least half of the flies with us.

October

At the end of three months, Marybeth was getting big enough to travel. I found a small apartment with kitchen privileges in Portsmouth, VA, which was just across the river from Norfolk. Betty and Marybeth came down to live in the apartment so I didn't have to make the trip every weekend and we could be together a lot more. I did a lot of switching watches and duty days with other fellows so that I could stand most of my watches during the day and then go home to the apartment overnight. The landlady we had was very nice.

Betty and Marybeth came to Portsmouth in August and stayed a month. One weekend the three of us went to Virginia Beach. We took a picture of Marybeth, who was about 3 months old, sitting by the ocean.

Soon thereafter, it was time for the ship dinner dance. Almost everyone planned on attending the event, held in a big hall downtown. The only ones who couldn't go were those who had the duty and had to stay aboard ship all night. Naturally, I was one of those fellows. However, I discovered that if I volunteered to be a shore patrol at the dance, I could go home to our apartment after the dance was over. So, that is what I did. In the beginning all we had to do was be there and see that everything went all right. But later in the evening after everyone had been drinking, things got a little rowdy.

Some fellows tried to dance with other fellows' wives and pretty soon one fight after another broke out. It didn't take long until we had a riot on our hands. We couldn't handle it and shore patrol and military police from all over showed up with "paddy wagons." They took the worst ones down to headquarters and put them in the brig. It was so bad that word was sent out to pick up any sailors from the Lind. It so happened that not everyone had gone to the dance.

Some fellows just went to the movies or maybe a bar and, wouldn't you know it, some of them coming out of a bar or a movie were walking down the street minding their own business and were stopped by some shore patrol and were asked what ship they were from and they said USS Lind. So they were hauled off to the brig, I understand that some of them put up a pretty good fight too; they didn't go peacefully.

As October came to an End, the ship was soon ready to leave good old Norfolk and head down to Cuba for training exercises. Of course that meant Betty and Marybeth had to leave and go back home. I took them back to Chester, said my farewells and hoped it wouldn't be long before I got word of a discharge.

November

We left for Cuba in early November and it was sort of a shakedown cruise to check out everything we had worked on in the yard. We went to our big Naval base in Panama, Guantanamo Bay. There we did a lot of gun firing at sleeves being towed by aircraft and all of the Sonarmen spent a lot of time ashore at the "attack teachers" which was a school for Sonarmen where we simulated attacks on submarines. This is why they were called attack teachers.

After several weeks of training at sea, making practice runs on real American submarines, we came to the end of November. We didn't have liberty off of the base but we were able to spend time at the enlisted men's club where we often sat drinking rum and Coco-Cola. It wasn't too bad.

Ducky Mohn and I and a few other fellows found out we were getting sent home for discharge. We received orders to pack and we were taken to the Naval air station where we were loaded on a Military Air Transport plane. It was loaded with a lot of boxes in the middle of the floor with the passengers sitting down both sides of the plane facing in towards the boxes, just like the plane we flew in to Japan.

We soon took off and we were told that we would be discharged at the Naval base in Jacksonville, FL. We leveled off at 10,000 feet when all of a sudden; we saw oil shooting out of one of the engines. Soon the pilot announced that we were turning around and would try to land. We landed safely and we were unloaded and put up in two barracks overnight while they worked on the engine.

Early the next morning they unloaded everything that was packed in the plane and then took the plane up for a trial run. I guess they figured everything was all right because when it landed they loaded everything back on and then they put us back on. We took off again and everything went all right and we had an uneventful trip to Jacksonville. Only some of us got off of the plane when we arrived in Jacksonville and the plane went on to Norfolk with the rest of the people. We were later told that the plane crashed while landing in Norfolk. We never found out how bad it was though.

Ducky and I were processed at the Jacksonville Naval Base and discharged on December 1, 1951. We were given money for transportation home and so far as I can remember, we went home by train.

Part V

77

Back from the Navy

Betty and Marybeth were still living in Chester with Betty's parents along with our dog, Butch. It was great to be home again and it was a time for many changes and decisions to be made. I asked myself things like, "Where were we going to live and did I still have a job?" We spent the month of December getting used to each other again and just enjoyed being together. My mother was still living on Pear Street in Reading and we went home to visit her soon after I got home.

I was relieved to find out that I still had a job with Textile Machine Works and that I could start working on January 7, 1952. I believe we managed to move back to Reading by that time or soon after.

We still had the old 1946 Chevrolet and it was a time of change for everyone. I was adjusting to being home after 18 months in the military and Betty was adjusting to having a baby and finally having her husband home. Betty and I set up housekeeping in our own first home and loved spending time with Marybeth who was 6 months old. It was great to be with Butch and my mother who lived with us for a while.

To refresh everyone's memory, when my brother and I got out of the service we were living in an apartment with our mother at 632 Schuylkill Avenue. We then found a home at 839 Pear Street. Ray and I bought the house 50-50 and the three of us moved in. That is where we lived while I was learning my trade at Textile Machine Works and going to Wyomissing Polytechnic Institute. At the same time Ray was going to Albright College and Penn State. Ray graduated from Albright in May of 1948 and then he took summer classes at Millersville College.

He took a teaching job at Warwick High School down towards Pottstown from September 1948 to June 1949. He then went to Penn State from June 1949 to June 1950. After I finished my trade and married Betty and went to North Carolina, we had someone live with our mother most of the time. I believe they moved in with my mother and me in the fall of 1949, about the time that Betty and I were married. I continued to live at home and work and Betty lived with her parents in Chester because we expected that I would get my orders any day to go out on the road, but unfortunately that took until the beginning of January.

So after we were married I kept running down to Chester every weekend to be with Betty. In the beginning of January I finally got my orders and we left for Franklin, North Carolina. I believe the Fraziers stayed with my mother until Ray finished classes at Albright around June of 1950. Then Ray found a lady by the name of Edith who lived with our mother until I was discharged from the Navy.

After Ray finished college he started teaching and eventually ended up in Philadelphia. That is where he met his future wife, Eva Flynn.

78
Back to Work

When I went back to work at Textile things had changed a lot. When I went back into the Navy in 1950 things were booming in the knitting machine business. But by now the circular seamless knitting machine came onto the market. It made one stocking at a time like a tube and had no seam. The full fashioned knitting machines made 30 stocking at a time. They were knitted flat and then seamed up the back and were made to the shape of the leg with fancy designs in them, which made them look a lot more attractive.

The problem was that the seamless were cheaper to make and also the women started to wear more slacks, shorts and dungarees. So all of a sudden the market for full fashioned stockings fell off tremendously. Needless to say there were not very many erector jobs to be had out on the road. Fortunately they were still putting up machines over at the Berkshire Knitting Mills right next door to the Textile Machine Works.

The Wyomissing Industries who owned Textile Machine Works owned the Berkshire Knitting Mills. They made the full fashioned knitting machines and braiding machines, which made nylon cord for things like parachute cord. The Berkshire Knitting Mills used the full fashioned knitting machines made by Textile and they were one of the largest knitting mills in the world. Wyomissing Industries also owned Narrow Fabric and they used the braiding machines to make the nylon cord and a lot of other fabrics.

I always enjoyed working at Berkshire building knitting machines. It was always interesting and challenging work and the fellows that I worked with were always very nice. The last two years of my trade I spent most of the time building knitting machines at Berkshire. Most of us were apprentices being trained by the two fellows who were in charge of installing the knitting machines. They were great fellows to work for and whenever an outside erector was between jobs on the road, they brought them in to work with us. It was a good experience because we learned a lot from them.

Having just returned from the Navy, I was happy to get a chance to work at Berkshire again. Only this time none of us were apprentices. All of us were old experienced erectors who used to work out on the road and worked in the Mill until we were called out. I really considered myself lucky to even be asked to work there considering that there weren't many jobs available in the industry. Some of the erectors didn't get that chance. They were sent to work back in the machine shop, which was less desirable and less money.

I had the opportunity to meet many of the old and experienced erectors and heard a lot of good stories about their experiences. I actually used to look forward to going to work and believe I enjoyed erecting more than any other job I ever had.

Soon after I was working again I bought a tan 1950 Chevrolet. It was like new and very nice looking. It was a two door with a sloped torpedo shaped back and it had a spotlight outside the driver's side window that you could control from a handle inside.

I remember many a weekend we loaded up the car and went back to Chester to visit Grammy and Pop Pop McBride. We had a nice car bed for Marybeth that fit in the back seat and most of the trips she slept most of the way down and back. That is one trait that I don't believe that she has lost!

79

Back to Textile

Around 1953 work started to get bad and most of us were sent back to Textile Machine Works to work in the shop. That meant a considerable drop in pay and it wasn't long before I realized that I wasn't going to be able to afford to keep my nice almost new Chevrolet. It broke my heart, but I advertised it in the paper and quickly found a buyer. Believe it or not, for the next two years we did without a car. I worked second shift most of that time which meant I could take a bus or trolley car to work. However, most of the time I had to walk home because it was too late for public transportation.

Working back in the shop was a big change from building knitting machines. I was in the milling department and most of it was piecework, but the rates were too high to make any money. The parts we machined were made of cast iron and that made it a pretty dirty job. After a few months I ended up with a bad skin condition. They sent me to the doctor and he said it was a breakdown of the fatty tissue from washing my hands so much and that before I washed my hands I should take most of the dirt off with mineral oil and then wash them. I followed doctor's orders and my hands slowly improved.

It was sort of a drag walking home late at night, especially in bad weather. One hot summer night I was walking home at 1 AM and a policeman stopped me. He asked me a lot of questions like who was I and where was I going and where I lived. I found out the next morning that a girl was murdered and they found her body in a trashcan about a block away on the next street over. As far as I know that murder was never solved.

80

Living on Pear Street

I'll never forget our neighbors on Pear Street. On the upper side of us were Mr. Harrison and Mrs. Rose Schwartz and their daughter Ruth who lived there until she got married. I think they had an older son and daughter also and both were married. Mr. Schwartz was a Bob Tailer, which meant he had his own bakery delivery route, and delivered bread and baked goods right to people's homes.

Our lower neighbor was Sarah Davenport, who lived with her parents across the street. When she married Stratton Yatron, they bought a house on our lower side. Sarah was a schoolteacher and Stratton and his family had a business selling and installing kitchen cabinets. Sarah and Stratton had a cat and I remember one time we were over visiting with them and the cat started chewing on an extension cord and all of a sudden let out a scream! She got a shock but was otherwise okay.

Across the street from Schwartz's was Irvin's grocery store and it was handy having one so close by. The Irvin's were old. Mr. Irvin, who was well up in years, and his son ran the store. The younger of the two Irvin's was Harry and he was married and had a son, Harry Jr., who later became a Methodist minister.

Next to the Irvin's lived Jack and Joan Bowman. They had a son whose name was Billy, and he was about Marybeth's age. Jack worked at the Continental Can Company and later took a job with Adam's Clothes. He soon became manager of his own store. Joan was a nurse but I'm not sure where she worked.

Next to them were Zimmer's who had three boys and two girls. Back on our side of the street, next to Yatron's, lived Red and Miriam Moyer and their son Kenny. Red worked at the American Casualty Insurance Company where Betty worked before I met her. He was a veteran of World War II and he was in the Rangers. He was hurt pretty bad in Italy during the Battle of Anzio.

Eventually he had his leg amputated. That didn't slow him down though and he was very active with the Boy Scouts. I liked to tell the story about a time he was with the Scouts at summer camp. After lights out when everyone was supposed to be in their tents sleeping, he heard there was going to be a walk through inspection by some of the big wigs. So, he took his artificial leg off and placed under the edge of the tent so that half of it stuck outside. Well, the inspector walked through and when he saw the leg protruding from the tent he gave it a good kick. To his surprise, the leg went quite a distance. Red never said what happened after that, but he got a kick telling the story!

We had garbage collection on Pear Street and we put our garbage can out at the curb in the evening and three times a week they came around with a big open truck and collect the garbage. That used to smell great on a hot summer night! You can only imagine what it sounded like with the banging of all of those garbage cans and lids.

We used to like to sit out on our front porch late at night and talk with the neighbors. Marybeth slept in a crib in the back bedroom, which was right at the top of the steps so we had to be pretty quiet so as not to wake her up.

We had a lot of bats in the neighborhood and every once in a while one got in the house. I don't know if they flew in the door when we walked in sometimes or if they got in someplace up in the attic, but every once in a while we found one flying around in the house. So I got my bat catching outfit, a hat and a broom, opened a door or a window and tried to chase it out. It never seemed to work too well. I remember one time I was chasing one in the living room and when I knocked it down and it went under the sofa and it laid there baring its teeth at me. One time the lady who lived three doors down woke up in the middle of the night with a bat lying on her chest!! Can you imagine how that felt?

One night when we were putting Marybeth to bed she stood up in her crib and said, "Look at the butterfly!" Just then a bat flew by and I was off for my bat catching outfit again!

81

Betty's Brother Buddy

Betty had a brother by the name of Francis William McBride. He was born about 1926 and had health problems from the time he was very young. I believe he had rheumatic fever or a rheumatic heart or both. As he was growing up he was always known as "Buddy." Because of his health, Betty's mother used to take her and her brother up to the Pocono's where they stayed on a farm outside of Tannersville for the summer.

Buddy had wanderlust and got in trouble now and then. At times he disappeared without even a goodbye.

During World War II he tried to join the Navy but he was turned down due to his health. Sometime later he took off without a word and no one knew where he went. Soon after that his draft notice came up, but since he wasn't around to sign up even though they probably wouldn't have taken him he automatically became a draft dodger. As time went by, every now and then an FBI agent stopped by the home of Betty's parents, just to see if they had ever heard from him.

By the time I met Betty in 1948, her brother had been gone about three years and they still didn't know where he was.

That all changed in the early summer of 1953 when Betty's parents received a birth announcement from Buddy. It was mailed from the state of Washington and it read:

210

Name: Frank William McBride
Birthday: May 22, 1953
Weight: 7 pounds 8 and 3/4 ounces
Parents: Sylvia and Frank

A note at the bottom of the announcement read, "I'm in good health. You'll be hearing from me again."

Later that summer we received a phone call from Betty's parents and her mother said Buddy showed up at their doorstep alone. He said his wife and baby were home in New York. Mom asked if they could come up to visit us and naturally we said yes. They soon arrived and I met Buddy for the first time. He seemed all right and we got along fine. They stayed at our house overnight.

During the years of 1953 and 1954 Betty had two miscarriages and then finally became pregnant with Steve somewhere around the beginning of August. In early October we had a big hurricane, Hazel, that went through Reading and did a lot of damage. It came up the east coast between October 8 and 16. Betty's baby doctor was Dr. Kring and his home and office was on the corner of North 5th and Windsor Streets and she had an appointment with him the evening the hurricane came through.

He was supposed to give her an injection for morning sickness, so I guess she felt that it was pretty important for her to go. We didn't have a car but decided to try to get to his office anyway. It wasn't raining at the time but the wind was blowing very hard and we decided to walk. However, we soon discovered there were trees and electric wires down here and there. So, we had to sort of weave around where ever it was possible to walk. The only thing in our favor was that there was no traffic! We got there and rang his doorbell and I guess we were the last people he expected to find at his door. His electricity was off and he greeted us with a lantern. Betty got her shot and we returned home without too much trouble.

After that I discovered that the wind blew over our TV antenna and it was hanging over the edge of the second floor roof between the two houses. I was afraid that it might come down and hurt someone or maybe go through one of the windows. So I went up on the roof and lashed it down with rope to secure it.

I grew up in St. Matthew's Lutheran Church at 5th and Elm Street and as Marybeth got older we started to take her to Sunday school. Sometime around 1954 I started to teach a class of young boys. That was quite an experience. I had never done it before but wanted to follow in my brother's footsteps. When I was about 15 my brother Ray taught a class of young boys about my age and I was included in his class.

82

Inspector

Towards the last half of 1954 I was transferred to the Boreamatic department to be an inspector. I don't think that it paid anymore, but it was on day shift and it was a welcome surprise. There were two other inspectors in that department, Paul Ireland and John Fidler. Paul was the first part inspector who checked the first part off the production line to insure that everything was right. John was much older than me and had been at Textile most of his life. I had never met him before but we discovered we were very distant cousins. He also had a twin brother working in the same department.

John and I worked side by side making sure that following the first inspection everything was all right. We circulated through the department and inspected parts as they came off various machines. Many things could go wrong with the machines and then the parts became scrap. It was a pretty interesting job and I got to meet a lot of different people.

I got to know Ken Adair who was an operator from Adamstown. He used to tell me about his part time job selling Cutco products. The company made kitchen knives of various sizes and shapes and carried a nice selection of carving and steak knives. They were made of very good steel and durable material and after talking to him for a number of days he talked me into selling Cutco products!

One evening he took me along to a meeting and introduced me to the top salesman. By the time I left the meeting I was signed up as a salesman and even had some products to take along with me. Our territory was unlimited and someone with a good gift of gab could make a fortune. However, I wasn't that gifted! I stuck with it for quite a while and worked hard selling some but when I ran out of friends and relatives business slowed down.

While I was working in the Boreamatic department I ran across an interesting situation. One of the jobs I had was inspecting needle bar arms that were used on the knitting machines. These arms had two half-inch holes bored through them with a very close tolerance. They wanted to hold the size of the hole to .500 plus or minus .0002. To check the holes that closely we used an air gauge which was an air hose with a probe on the end that we slid into the half-inch hole. There were two tiny holes in the probe that let air pass through and the closer the fit of the hole around the probe the less air passed through. The amount of air passing through the probe showed up on a gauge controlling a float inside a glass tube. The float had to stay within two designated lines and if it didn't the part was thrown away as scrap.

When I saw what they were doing I really had to laugh! The reason for this was that when I was out on the road building knitting machines with Sam McPherson we got bulletins from Textile telling us about some things to look for. I clearly remembered one referring to this particular needle bar arm. It stated that before we assembled them on the machine we should make sure to take a reamer and run it through those particular holes a couple times to make them bigger.

Evidently they were having a lot of trouble with those arms freezing up after the machine ran a while and here we were in the shop throwing away good arms because they were a little big in those holes. Right away I went to the foreman and explained the situation. He went and checked it out and discovered that I was right and after that they did away with the air gauge. They should have given me a bonus because I really saved them a lot of money! I never even got a thank you, though.

As time went by I became a little unhappy working in the shop. I would have sooner been out on the road building knitting machines but of course there weren't that many jobs available. Shop work didn't pay well so I decided to go see the Personnel Director, Mr. Flieschman, about getting a raise. When I asked him he said, "My god, you are already getting more than anyone else in the department." I then explained that I didn't see how that could be possible because the man working right next to me was John Fidler and that he was there much longer then I was. He said, "Yes, and he is getting a nickel an hour less than you are." After a little more discussion he asked me how much I was earning per hour and I told him $1.99. He said "Well, I'll give you $2 an hour but that's the best I can do." Well, you can imagine how that made me feel!

Soon after that I decided to talk to Mr. Duff who was in charge of the erectors. I eventually got to talk to his secretary and told him how I felt and asked him if there wasn't anything available out on the road right now. I told him if there wasn't I would have to look around for something else. The following Monday I was called over to his office and he asked me if I could leave for Mexico by the following Friday.

Of course I said yes! While I was in the office a Textile servicemen by the name of Bill Marshal stopped in to see Mr. Bentz. He handled Mexico and South America and when he found out I was going to Mexico he told me to get a haircut before I left because the barbers weren't too good down there.

I was busy that week! I had to get a letter from the Police department stating that I never was arrested or had a record. I had to go to Philadelphia to get a working permit for Mexico as well as get a passport. The worst part was when we found out that Betty wouldn't be able to go along because she was pregnant. The airlines would not take passengers after they were so many months along in their pregnancy. Also, about this time she developed Phlebitis and had to stay off of her legs as much as possible.

I finally left Reading on Saturday January 29, 1955. I took the train to New York City and checked into the Peter Cooper Hotel. I decided to try to look up Betty's brother, Buddy, who was living in Greenwich Village and after walking about 20 blocks, I found him! We talked a little while and when he finally remembered me, we went across the street to a bar and had a couple bottles of beer. We talked for about two hours and then I decided I'd better head back to the hotel. I caught a cab back to the hotel and then I talked to Betty on the phone before I went to bed. I told her about my visit with Buddy and how we talked about his paintings and upcoming shows.

83

Mexico

On Sunday January 30, I took a cab at 9:30 in the morning out to the Idelwild Airport that later became the Kennedy Airport. Since I hadn't traveled much by air except in the Navy I was quite impressed with the airport. Keep in mind that it was 1955 and it was fascinating seeing airlines from so many different countries and to see and hear so many people of different nationalities.

I flew on a big shiny new Air France plane that came from Paris and was going to Mexico City nonstop. The nice part was that I was flying first class where the seats were spacious and the service was great. We had a great flight. The weather was perfect, and the food was something else. They served us cocktails before the meal, champagne with dinner and wine with our dessert. Later we enjoyed tea and cookies. It was a real treat!

We arrived in Mexico City about 8:20 Eastern standard time and it took me about one and half hours to get through the red tape of immigration.

Roy Lape, the fellow that I would be working with, and his wife met me at the airport. They seemed like very nice people and they brought me to the Hotel Geneve. I believe they might have been about 15 or 20 years older than I was.

They got me checked in and I got a room about as big as our bedroom at home with a private bathtub, shower, washbowl, and toilet. It was nicely furnished and cost 35 pesos, which amounted to $2.80 in American dollars. It also had a phone and the place seemed very clean.

Roy and his wife arrived several weeks earlier in their brand new 1955 Chevrolet that they had driven down from the United States. They told me that when they crossed the border into Mexico they had to pay quite a large deposit of money that they would get back when they left Mexico with the car. I guess this was to discourage them from selling the car while they were in Mexico.

My tools arrived on a later plane and that Monday morning we had to go back to the airport and pick them up on the way to work. We spent our workdays at the plant, Media Perfecta.

We always drove to work with Roy's car. It wasn't a bad drive because it only took 15 or 20 minutes. A lot of women were out early sweeping their sidewalks and they usually wore a mask over their nose and mouth for protection from the dust. There weren't many traffic lights, but at some of the big intersections there was a platform in the middle of the intersection with a policeman standing on it directing traffic. However, most of the intersections didn't have traffic lights or policemen. The first car to the intersection went, providing you had a loud enough horn and a little nerve. It was amazing that there weren't more accidents.

Sometimes we saw fellows riding bicycles with enormous baskets filled with baked goods on top of their heads. Once in a while they dropped a basket full into the street and stopped to pick up the baked goods and be on their way. We also saw people delivering milk on bicycles.

Since Roy had already started to work there a week or so before I arrived we followed his schedule. We started work at 7, so we had to get up early. We ate breakfast at the hotel and Roy told me he had discovered that the hotel kitchen made the lunches for the Air France airline every day. So he talked them into making lunches for us too! They also fixed us a thermos of cold water to take along to work. The only drinking water they had at the plant was a big 5 or 10 gallon bottle of spring water or at least they said it was spring water. At noon we usually went back to the hotel to eat our lunch. Roy had his with his wife and I usually ate in my room.

The plant had about a dozen machines running and we were building two more. They received the two new machines completely torn down and packed in boxes, so we had about a half dozen young fellows helping us. It was mostly their job to unpack everything with our supervision and then to clean everything because most of the parts were covered with Cosmoline, a protective coating to keep them from rusting. The interesting part was that none of them spoke a word of English and we didn't speak any Spanish but we got along fine with sign language and it wasn't too long before we started to pick up some Spanish. They were all very young and they got paid about six or seven pesos a day. That amounted to about a dollar a day in our money and that was for a ten hour day. I believe the knitters were paid more because they were strong Union workers.

If the electricity went off for a while and didn't come back on within an hour, they went home for the rest of the day and got paid for it. It wasn't uncommon for the power to go off and Roy and I checked

217

to see what was causing it. We discovered they were using circular fuses and we could rotate it to the next setting. It was good for six different positions. A couple times we found out that someone took the fuse out and put a copper coin in place of it. That certainly wasn't the safest thing to do!

The plant was relatively clean and the people were very friendly. The owners were the only ones who spoke English and they didn't show up much.

We worked ten hours a day and about six to eight hours on Saturday. During the week we worked 7 to 12 and then went back to the hotel for lunch and then worked from 1 to 6. After work we went back to the hotel, took a shower and then Roy, his wife and I would go out to eat dinner around 7. Most of the Mexicans took a siesta after the noon meal and then worked late and ate dinner late, like about 8 or 9 in the evening. We rotated restaurants so that we got a variety of food and there were a lot of good restaurants within walking distance of the hotel. We enjoyed dinners from around the world including French, Swiss, and Italian food.

Soon after I arrived in Mexico I wrote to Betty every day or so whenever I had time. I missed her and Marybeth and I was anxious to hear how they both were making out. That was a new experience with Betty, having to take care of everything around the house, including tending the fire in the furnace. We had a coal furnace for heat and a bucket a day stove that heated the water. The bucket a day stove was just a small little coal stove next to the furnace that just heated the water and it just needed a bucket of coal a day. It was tricky to maintain it enough to have heat and hot water and to be able to cut it back at night so that it wouldn't burnout by morning.

February 2 I received my first letter from Betty, so she must have started writing soon after I left. Two days later I received another letter from her and by February 7 she started to receive letters from me regularly. Betty said that she and Marybeth went to Sunday school and that Marybeth was going to be in a talent show. She also sent news clippings about the cold weather and all of the snow they were getting. I guess I got out of Reading just in time.

Hotel Geneve was on the outskirts of Mexico City near the beautiful Chapultepec Park. A few blocks from the hotel was the home of the American Ambassador and we often walked past it going to or coming from one of the restaurants. About five or six blocks from the hotel was a big wide three-mile boulevard. It started at Chapultepec Park and went all the way downtown through the center of Mexico

City. Once we got out to the boulevard we could grab a cab for one peso or about eight cents.

The cabs ran up and down the length of the boulevard and all we had to do was hold up one finger and if he had room the driver stopped even though there might be other passengers in the car. You paid him one peso and when you got near where you were going he stopped and let you out. The other travel option was the trolley car. Although it was cheaper it was usually jam- packed. Sometimes passengers had to hang on the outside and the trolley never fully stopped. It only slowed down and passengers had to hop on or off.

Mexico City is about 7400 feet above sea level and I struggled with the altitude change for a week or two. I found myself getting extra tired, especially when I did some heavy lifting.

The employee restroom at the plant was dirty and didn't have regular toilet paper. Instead they used pieces of newspaper that they just threw in the corner because it was too heavy to flush down the toilet. They shoveled it out about once a week and that got to smell a little bit to say the least! It didn't take long for us to discover there was a private toilet for the owners and the office personnel. We got permission to use it but we couldn't get the key until the office started at 8 AM. So if you had to go before that you had a problem.

Most of the restaurants were within walking distance from the hotel so I got a chance to see various parts of the neighborhood. Right away I noticed the construction of their sidewalks. They were made of square concrete blocks with spaces between them to keep the sidewalks from cracking during earthquakes. Evidently that made the sidewalks more flexible and prevented damage. I also saw some people huddling around open fires at new construction sites.

Roy explained that night watchmen and their families camped on the grounds of the property they were overseeing and that's what we were witnessing. Another time I noticed what looked like a mailman sitting down on the curb along the sidewalk; he seemed to be holding some of the letters up in the air and staring at them. Roy said that he was looking for money in the letters. Truly, this was a new way of life!

I also had to get used to the fact that people weren't bashful in Mexico. If they had to go to the bathroom, they just went on the side of the road without any self- consciousness.

Soon after I arrived in Mexico, Bill Marshall stopped by to visit us. He was staying at the Hotel Reforma near the center of town. It was much bigger and newer than the Hotel Geneve and he invited us to have dinner with him. Although Roy and his wife had another engagement, I accepted and I went that evening because he was leaving the next day for South America. We ate in the dining room of his hotel and enjoyed cocktails and a delicious lobster tail dinner. Mexican singers serenaded us. It didn't cost me a cent because he put it on his charge account. I was also happy for the weekend because I didn't have to get up early in the morning.

In order to get paid Roy and I made out weekly time sheets, which were then signed by the plant owner and mailed to Textile. When I left Reading I was given $1,000 in traveler's checks to cover my expenses. I was allowed $75 a week for living expenses, which would ultimately be deducted from the $1,000 when we finished the job. I would have to return any leftover money and if I spent over that I would have to pay the difference myself.

I heard stories about some erectors who purposely overspent their allowance and because they owed so much money to the company they were sent out on the road so that they could pay it back. Meanwhile other erectors had to go back in the shop because there weren't enough outside jobs. I don't know how true that was but I wouldn't be surprised.

Anyway, we worked about 50 or 60 hours a week but only turned in 40 to 50 hours and saved about ten hours a week. We were allowed to do this so that when we finished our job and went home we had several weeks' time sheets accumulated and we could enjoy an extra paid vacation. Although it seemed like a good idea at the time, we were actually losing our overtime! Anyway, that was our regular pay and it was sent home to Betty. I lived on the weekly $75 expense allowance and since living in Mexico was so cheap I made out pretty good.

My hotel bill was only $2.80 a day $19.60 a week and meals were inexpensive too. Breakfast was about $.48, lunch $.25 and a steak dinner cost me anywhere from $1.00 to $1.25. Although American cigarettes were $.50 a pack, haircuts were only $.16 and a bottle of Coke was $.03. Trolley and bus fare was $.02 and taxi fare was $.08(one peso). My biggest expenses were laundry and the telephone bills. I used to call Betty regularly and that ran about one dollar a minute. Although we wrote back and forth every couple days I looked forward to the calls and it was worth it just to hear Betty's and Marybeth's voices.

You remember that I talked about working with Frank Ramos from Mexico when I was working at the Berkshire Knitting Mill? I did some checking to see how far he was from Mexico City and discovered a one-way trip took 14 hours by train or auto and 7 hours to fly. I decided not to make the trip.

One Saturday I went downtown by myself and decided to go to a movie. I didn't realize it until I got inside that it was a French picture with Spanish subtitles! Although I couldn't understand either I finally got the drift and enjoyed it.

Around Sunday noontime I was down at the front desk paying my hotel bill when Roy and his wife came along. They were on their way out to dinner and invited me to go along. We had a great time and then drove around town a little while. Eventually we visited a friend of theirs who was married and had four children. They were a Mexican family of German descent and lived in a large home surrounded by a wall. They had a few servants and housekeepers and talked about how the hired help was very organized and belonged to a union. After a nice visit we returned to the hotel.

Some evenings we sat in the hotel lobby after dinner and had the chance to meet some interesting people. One time I talked to the gentleman next to me and he turned out to be Earl Stanley Gardener. He was a writer of murder mysteries and was a very interesting fellow. Another evening the Lapes invited me to go with them to visit a couple they knew from Reading. They had two children and he was a fixer, the mechanic that works on the knitting machines in a hosiery mill. He worked in one of the mills in Mexico City.

His name was Jerry Youse and his wife was raised in the 700 block of Gordon Street in Reading. That was about a block away from where I was born. She knew a lot of people I knew. They seemed like very nice people and I enjoyed talking about home with her. They lived in a beautiful house with two maids and even had a television. That gave me the chance to experience Mexican TV with their 3 channels. The picture wasn't very clear and even though the Mr. District Attorney show was in Spanish I enjoyed it any way. I also got to watch Laurel and Hardy in English.

Roy and I kept on schedule back at the plant. We were each building knitting machines that faced each other with an isle down the middle. We put the frames together and installed shafts and other parts which added a lot more weight to it. It was our responsibility to make sure the machines were straight, positioned properly and perfectly level.

I worked with some fine young fellows but they had the bad habit of bumming cigarettes all of the time. Yes, I smoked cigarettes regularly and American cigarettes cost $.52 a pack. Mexican cigarettes were only $.05 a pack but tasted horrible! I couldn't afford to pay for 7 of us smoking American cigarettes. One evening I decided to buy a pack of Mexican cigarettes and one morning I put the American cigarettes in my pocket and the Mexican cigarettes on top of my toolbox. When they came to ask me for a cigarette I pointed towards my toolbox and said, "Help yourself." That was the end of their bumming cigarettes!

I think I mentioned before that the American Embassy was just around the corner from my hotel. Well, it also turned out to be the home of the American Ambassador to Mexico. On February 9, Vice President Nixon came to visit the Ambassador and the neighborhood was crawling with police. The next evening we ate at a restaurant near the hotel just across the street from the American Ambassador's home. Just as we came out of the restaurant 10 motorcycle police started up their motors. They had closed off the block to traffic and someone said that Vice President Nixon was getting ready to leave. As we stood there, sure enough, Mr. Nixon and his wife came out and got in a big black car with a procession of cars and motorcycle police. We stood right across from the driveway as his car pulled out and Mr. Nixon and his wife actually waved at us, so we waved back.

The Hotel Geneve was one of the older hotels but it was very nice and very clean. It also was heated and had hot water, which was a luxury some hotels didn't offer their guests. Our hotel had a good reputation and many of the older tourists stayed there.

The hotel laundry service was efficient and very reasonable. My laundry bill usually amounted to $1.40 in American currency. That wasn't bad for a week's laundry that included everything but my work dungarees. They got so dirty that I didn't even bring them back to the hotel. Instead, I gave them to one of my helpers and he took them home for his mother to wash for 3 pesos or 24 cents in our money. The laundry at the hotel was done up nicely. However, you might get a laugh out of this though. When I sent the pants home with my helper it was usually a week before he returned them and even then they were still damp. One day I questioned him about it; he told me that when he took them home his mother washed them then his brother wore them all week. She then washed them again and he brought them back to work. Ha!! What could I say for 3 pesos?

Soon after I arrived in Mexico I asked Betty to have the Reading Eagle newspaper sent to me so that I could keep up with the news from home. I started to receive them regularly but with working

10 hours a day and trying to write to Betty every day I hardly had time to read the paper. I also wrote to Marybeth, my mother, my brother Ray, Reverend Siegart, Frank Ramos, Roma, Eleanor, Mr. & Mrs. Willis, the Moyers, Yatrons, Mr. & Mrs. Schwartz, Mohn, Moll, and Walter and Mary Frantz. That was enough to give me writer's cramps!

Eventually Roy and I started carrying our lunch to work instead of going back to the hotel to eat at noon. I made the suggestion because we lost an hour and a half every day going back to the hotel for lunch. We figured that by eating lunch at work, we gained 9 hours a week per paycheck and that brought us up to 64 hours per week. We found out that the mill was closing down over Holy Week (Easter was April 10) and I wanted to do this in order to make up the time that we would lose shutting down that week. So if we worked 64 hours a week and turned in only 55 hours a week it made up for the pay we missed during Holy Week.

The Lapes had some friends who owned a restaurant around the corner from the hotel. However, they gave that up to try their hands at the chicken raising business. They lived out in the country where the Lapes visited them regularly. They usually went on a Sunday morning and one time they invited me to go along. When we arrived we ate breakfast there and paid for it just like we were eating in a restaurant. We could order whatever we wanted and they prepared each meal individually. Breakfast was delicious!

Evidently when the city restaurant business got on his nerves they gave it up. Later on they bought a place out in the country with the intention of making it into a restaurant. But because it was so far off of the main road it didn't work out. So instead they decided to raise chickens and run a casual eatery. Many of their friends and old customers drove out to the country to enjoy a made-to-order home cooked meal for a reasonable price.

Back at the plant we built the Reading 100, a 60 gauge machine, which was a finer gauged machine where the needles were closer together so as to produce a finer material. That made the machines a lot more sensitive and for down in Mexico that wasn't too good. The machines had to be extra straight and level and because Mexico City sat on an old lakebed, the buildings were settling or sinking at the rate of two inches to two feet a year at some places! There were many buildings that looked like the Leaning Tower of Pisa.

By the time Valentine's Day rolled around I was feeling down about being away from home. Being out on the road wasn't all it was cracked up to be. Although it paid well it was rough being away from my family for so long.

It had been pretty hard on Betty since I left for Mexico. She had to take care of all of the things I always took care of such as paying the bills. She was pretty good with it though and had no problems setting up a budget and sticking to it. The biggest challenge was running the house and looking after Marybeth while being pregnant. I am sure there were many times when she didn't feel that great and would just as soon rest and not do much of anything. However she had a peppy little 4-year old to take care of, so that didn't happen very often. But even in the midst of all of this she managed to write me just about every day and kept me updated about Marybeth and all that was going on at home. Her letters really kept my spirits up. I know it was time consuming because sometimes her letters were six to eight pages long!

On top of all of this Betty taught the Mother's class in Sunday school. That couldn't be too easy either. Speaking of Sunday school, she mentioned in one of her letters that she hadn't driven the car much since I left for Mexico. However, one Sunday she decided to take the car to church. She said that it felt so strange and that when she turned on the key, pulled out the hand throttle and the choke and tread on the gas, nothing happened. She tried it again and still nothing happened. Then Marybeth said, "Push the button, you didn't push the button" and sure enough, Betty had forgotten to push the starter button! (For you younger people, back in the old days cars had hand throttles, chokes, starter buttons and a lot of other weird things.) Betty said that it felt strange to be behind the wheel again but after that she didn't have any trouble.

At the end of February Betty wrote to let me know that Eva Flynn's mother had passed away and that she felt bad about not being able to go to the funeral because there wouldn't be anyone there from Raymond's side of the family. Also she found out that they had put my mother in bed in the infirmary to keep her off of her feet to see if it would help her ulcerated leg to heal. The worst news was that Betty had a blood clot in her leg and she had to stay off of her leg as much as possible.

It was an awful time for me to be away when she needed me. She decided to go home to her parents in Chester for a while so they could take care of her and Marybeth. That made me feel a lot better but I guess her mother was thinking it was about time I started staying home when Betty was pregnant. So, Betty and Marybeth stayed in

Chester with Mom and Pop for a while. Betty told me in her letter that before she left Reading she canceled the newspaper, the Lutheran magazine and the milkman delivery. She pulled out all the plugs, turned off the water and let the fires go out.

The Lapes had two married children as well as two grandchildren and their daughter was expecting in April. Mrs. Lape belonged to the Eastern Star and when the Shrine had a Mardi Gras they invited me to go along to see it with them. It was more like a banquet, but the meal wasn't that much to speak of. I guess they cut down on the meal so as to make more money. They had seven girls at the party who were princesses from different colleges in Mexico and the United States.

Each one drew a ball out of a basket and the one who drew the gold ball became Queen of the Mardi Gras. They also had a "Grab Bag" where we bought a ticket to win a prize. I won a jar of Heinz onions and a jar of some kind of seasoning. I couldn't use them, so I gave them to Mrs. Youse and then she gave me something that she won that I could take home for Betty. It was a basket that was hung on the wall and held flowers or vines in it. I don't know what it was called, but it was sort of cute.

By the end of February I knew that I would be home in a few months. I called Betty to tell her the news and our eight-minute conversation cost me $8! At that rate it wouldn't take long for me to own the telephone company!

I called Betty on my birthday, March 2, and she said that her left leg was very painful and still hurt when she tried to walk on it. She said she could move around in bed pretty easy and most of the swelling had gone down. She also told me she had to put our dog Butch to sleep. He attacked a little dog that lived a few doors from Mom and Pop and Betty had to hit him with a broomstick to break it up. She was fearful about having an untrustworthy dog around the new baby and decided that it would be best to have him put to sleep. I know it was a hard decision for her to make. Butch was our first dog, but I understood that it had to be done, and I was proud of her for making that difficult decision. On top of all of this Betty was having trouble giving Marybeth her medicine. Evidently Marybeth didn't like the medicine and wouldn't take it. Even Grammy Mac couldn't get it in her.

On March 4 I received a phone call from Frank Romas from northern Mexico who used to work with me at Berkshire. He had just arrived in Mexico City for a visit and wanted to get together. We made arrangements to meet for dinner the following evening. We met at a nice restaurant and enjoyed a delicious dinner and great conversation reminiscing over old times when we worked together in Reading.

We were in the restaurant quite a while when all of a sudden Frank said to me, "We have already paid the bill, let us leave now. Stick with me and don't hold back or stop." We were out of there in a flash and fortunately a taxi pulled up and whisked us away. When I asked him what that was all about he said he overheard the three Mexicans sitting next to us say they were planning to rob us when we got outside. So...we made our getaway just in time!

On Sunday morning the Lapes invited me to go with them and their friend, Dr. Streeter, out for breakfast at the home of their friends in the country. Then we drove from there down to Cuernavaca, which was a town about an hour and a half away from Mexico City. Many rich Americans owned big homes and ranches there. It was about 2,500 feet lower then Mexico City and many people who minded the altitude in Mexico City went down to Cuernavaca for the weekend. It was much hotter down there and I got a little sunburn on my face that day. Because it was market day we went through the streets' markets and I picked up a few souvenirs. I bought a dress for Marybeth and hoped it would fit her when I returned home.

It was a beautiful drive down to Cuernavaca. Mexico City is 7,500 feet above sea level and we had to drive over a mountain 10,000 feet high and then down to Cuernavaca, which is only 5,000 feet high. We used to think Clingmans Dome was high at 6,000 feet in North Carolina but it was nothing compared to this! We went through the Palace of Cortes, which was built in 1523. Inside was a beautiful mural by the famous Mexican painter Diego Rivera. We also saw the ruins of an Aztec temple consisting of five terraces 400 feet high. It was an amazing sight to see.

Dr. Streeter was a very interesting man who the Lapes had known for 14 years. He used to own a hospital in Chicago and one day he decided to retire and gave the hospital to his employees and he traveled ever since. He was quite knowledgeable and Roy and I learned more from him about Mexico than I had the last five weeks living there.

At the end of the day he walked me to my hotel room and he was surprised to discover that I was in room number 251. Ironically he said that when he first met me I reminded him of a young fellow who was the son of a close friend of his, a Dr. Marker. It so happened that this Dr. Marker had room 251 for about 10 years during the time he developed the medicine Cortisone. That was pretty amazing!

I was happy to receive a letter from Betty saying that her leg was getting better and that she hoped to move back to Reading in April. I wrote to her to say that she better not push it and do too much or she would be back in bed again. Soon after that I received another letter saying it was worse again and that she had to stay off of her feet. So, she wasn't going back to Reading early and I felt better knowing that she would be with Mom and Pop in case she had any problems. If she went back to Reading she would have to start shoveling coal again and that wouldn't be good for her in the condition that she was in.

One morning while doing laundry, Betty's mother discovered the clothes dryer was smoking like a house on fire and filled the house with the smell of burnt rubber. She called the fire company and before they came a policeman arrived. By the time he arrived the machine had stopped smoking and it had also blown a fuse. The fire truck arrived and four firemen paraded into the house and looked the situation over. They decided it was safe and all she had to do was air the place out and call the repairman. Unfortunately the next day there was a screech of brakes out front and they found out that a little boy from up the street got hit. Evidently he ran out from behind a truck right into the path of a car coming down the street. Pop went to help the boy and was relieved that he wasn't hurt too badly. During that time Betty mentioned that the baby sure made its presence known because it was kicking the dickens out of her!

Betty received a letter from our friend Elsie Banke who told her that she had a date with Ed on Saturday evening and they went to the movies and then to a nice restaurant for dinner. She thought it looked pretty serious with them. Betty said she would like to see her get married, especially to someone real nice.

On March 13 the hotel dining room was quite full for breakfast and a young man asked me if it was alright if he sat at my table. He turned out to be a Canadian fellow from Montreal. He was real friendly and we talked quite a bit. I told him that I knew some people living in Montreal and we discovered that he had some close friends who lived across the street from the McPhersons. Small world, huh?

Later that morning I went on a sightseeing tour. A licensed guide picked us up at the hotel and our party consisted of an elderly couple from Detroit and a Japanese fellow from Tokyo. There were usually five in the party besides the guide but we only had four so the guide stopped by his house and took his wife along. I thought that was thoughtful of him. The guide was very nice and he spoke English very well. He told us that he had just won the lottery for 100,000 pesos! When other guides saw him they told their party, "There is the man that won all the money."

The tour was real nice for $12 and we saw many beautiful places. Our first stop was the Palace of Fine Arts. It was made of marble and was so heavy that it had sunk into the ground 9 feet over the past 40 years. Fortunately it wasn't cracked because it sank as one piece. Where you used to go up the steps into the palace you now went down the steps.

The stage inside the auditorium had a glass curtain that weighed 22 tons! It is the only one in the world and it was made up of millions of tiny pieces of different colored glass formed into a beautiful picture of the two famous volcanoes in Mexico. They did a light show on the glass mosaic curtain that showed how the night turns to dawn and how the rising sun progressed into broad daylight. It was very beautiful.

After we left the Palace of Fine Arts we went across the street to the National Cathedral. It was built in the 1500's and the outside looked as if it was falling apart. The inside, however, was filled with beautiful three dimensional paintings and everything was trimmed in gold.

We then went to the Floating Gardens, which is considered the Venice of Mexico. We took a boat ride along a waterway where the boats were trimmed with flowers. Other boats were filled peddlers who sold flower blankets and all sorts of souvenirs. There were even some boats with groups of musicians on them playing music for the other boats. It was a wonderful experience!

Next we went to a fine restaurant for dinner. I enjoyed a delicious ham dinner covered with thick slices of pineapple. Because there was a lot of distance between these places we visited we got to see a lot of the beautiful countryside. It reminded me a lot like the farmland where I used to deliver newspapers only more up and down rolling hills.

After dinner we went to see a bull fight. It started at 4PM and it was said to be the only thing in Mexico that started on time. Sure enough, at the stroke of four the parade of the matadors preceded the bull fight. One had to be sort of bloodthirsty to thoroughly enjoy it. The bull ring was filled to capacity and held 60,000 people. They killed six bulls and each one took about 20 minutes. I think I took two rolls of film trying to capture their cultural tradition.

A few times I went bowling at the Swiss Club with Roy and his wife. Roy was a member of the Shrine and they always have a get-together the third Tuesday of the month at the club. They served us dinner and then we did some bowling. Whenever something crazy happened in Mexico people had the habit of saying that it can only happen in Mexico. Well, I was beginning to agree with them. I met a man that night that told me about an unfortunate traveling experience.

He took a train to another city in Mexico and during his return the train ran out of fuel in the middle of nowhere. So they sat for two hours and waited for a relief engine to tow them to Mexico City. Well, the engine finally came and it so happened their train was sitting on a curve and the relief engine ran right into his train head on and then jumped the track! At that point both engines were badly damaged and so they waited longer for help. Pretty soon a train from Texas came along and nearly hit them as well. Soon after that a train came along from the opposite direction and it had to stop too. Things were pretty well tied up and no one seemed to know what to do. Eventually someone came along with some horses and the man I was talking to got on a horse and rode with suitcases in hand for two hours to a bus station. So much for public transportation! It could only happen in Mexico.

Eventually Roy and I were asked to go over to the mill next door. Our job was to re-level their machines. We did, and it was quite a job. By the time we finished we had thin pieces of cardboard under the machines at one end and almost four-inch blocks at the other end to compensate for the lopsided sinking of the building!

After being in Mexico for seven weeks it finally rained. It was just a short shower though, not even enough to settle the dust. Still it was nice to see rain.

That day I decided to go out to do some shopping. I ended up buying a miniature dog made of onyx, which is something Mexico is noted for. I then ate dinner at the Hotel Reforma and went to a movie near the hotel. I saw Rogue Cop starring Robert Taylor and because it was in English I had a great time. One good thing about the movies down there was that no matter how good the picture was the most they could charge was 32 cents and after it had been running a couple weeks it dropped to 24 cents.

The following day I decided to go for a walk around the neighborhood close to my hotel. I ran across a big outside farmer's market. It was just as big as the one we had back home at Reading Fairgrounds only much dirtier. Because they didn't use refrigeration, some of the fly infested meat hanging out smelled pretty bad. I did manage to buy a tablecloth with napkins and a pretty apron, though.

Betty sent me a package for my birthday and the post office told me that I could pick it up but I would have to pay $14 duty on it in American money. Betty had told me that the shirt wasn't worth a lot and she had bought it on sale, so after a little thought I told them to return it to the sender.

The last letter that I received from Betty was dated March 19 and she said that she and her mother went shopping for a coat for Marybeth. Luckily they found a coat, hat, and bag that suited both Mom and Betty. Marybeth liked it too! Mom found a dress for

Marybeth and they gave it to her for an Easter present. Betty said in her letter that she wanted Marybeth's picture taken as soon as possible in her new outfit because she really looked out of this world! She said that the coat was gray with a wide collar and had 4 pleats in the back. It cost $18.98 but it was what they called a Grow Coat and she should be able to wear it next year.

Her hat was a lacy looking affair that sat right on top of her head. It had a little velvet ribbon hanging down the back and a spray of tiny pink roses across the front. Her dress was a very pretty shade of pink nylon trimmed with a little lace around the collar and a sash. It had an under slip (which could be worn as a sundress in hot weather) of printed nylon (pink and blue roses) that showed through the pink dress. The whole outfit went together so well she was really a picture in it. The hat and bag were $3.69 and Mom paid $9 for the dress. Betty said that they let her try the whole thing on together when they got home and could hardly get the things off of her!

On March 23 Frank Ramos called and said that he wanted to talk to me because he was still in Mexico City looking for a job. We got together that night and had dinner at my hotel. Later we sat in the cocktail lounge drinking beer and talking until about 11:30. I told him I would put in a good word for him because the owners were looking for a fixer for another mill they owned in another part of town. They interviewed him and gave him a job!

Betty and I had been discussing where the best place to have the baby would be. Her legs were better and she was thinking seriously of moving back home to Reading. After weighing the pros and cons of moving or staying, Betty decided it was best if she had the baby in Chester where she could be with her parents. She wanted to have the baby at the Chester Hospital because she always liked Dr. Neimitz, the doctor she had when Marybeth was born. I felt relieved that she decided to stay in Chester. I hoped to be home before the baby arrived but I didn't like the idea of her being alone in Reading.

Betty was seeing Dr. Kring in Reading. Since Pop worked during the week, they made the doctor's appointment for Sunday, March 27. In her letter, Betty mentioned one thing that happened on her trip. She said that on the way to Reading they were going up the Morgantown Road and were about half way when all of a sudden she felt sick and had to throw up.

Her Dad stopped the car and she got out and lost her breakfast. She said that when she threw up, usually her bladder was uncontrollable too. So, there she was with both ends going. There were no cars going by and the nearest house was down the hill a way, so she took her pants off right there beside the car. She said fortunately that is all that got wet. Later she said she remembered that there had been a strong smell of gasoline on their way up to Reading and that was probably what made her sick. They were carrying a can of gasoline in the car and they discovered that it leaked a little bit sometimes.

When Betty talked to the doctor he told her that the baby should be due about May 9th. I guessed it was about time that I get home.

About a week before, the sole of one of my shoes came loose so Mrs. Lape took it to the shoemaker for me and he stitched it up for 16 cents. Then a few days later the tongue fell out so she took it back and he sewed it back in for 4 cents. (Weren't those prices something?)

231

Well, there it was the start of April. It wouldn't be too much longer and we would be heading home.

Just before I was going out for supper the phone rang and it was Frank Romas. He said that he was down in the lobby so I went down and we had supper together and then we sat and talked in the lobby until about 11 o'clock. He had come over to say goodbye. He was going back home for most of April and then he would come back to Mexico City. He was taking that job I got him as fixer at the other mill, but he wouldn't be starting until May first. I hoped that he would make out all right.

The next week was Holy Week and I had hoped that I would be able to work that week, but I wasn't able to. I talked to the owner of the mill and he said that everything would be closed up tight and that he would rather not have me work. I explained to him why I wanted to get finished as soon as possible because I needed to get home before the baby arrived and he said, "Well, if it's that important and you really want to come in and work you can but I would rather you not because there won't be any heat and maybe not even any power."

On top of all of that, Roy Lape told me he thought that I shouldn't work that following week. He didn't want to work that week because he and his wife were going down to Acapulco for three or four days. Acapulco was the Atlantic City of Mexico. It really was supposed to be a paradise where all of the American movie stars went. Roy said, "If you work next week, Ken, and I don't then Textile will want to know why!" I really hadn't thought of that before, but it was true. I heard stories of fellows catching hell for that same reason. It probably would have been all right for me but it would have looked bad for Roy.

It made me mad and we argued about it for a while, but in order to keep peace in the family I agreed not to work that next week. After all, he was supposed to be in charge of that little operation. We finally did come to terms. He would be back from Acapulco on Wednesday and then we would both work on Thursday. Then we would take the rest of the week off. It really wasn't as bad as it sounded. I was much further along than I had expected to be by this time and should have my machine running 6 days after we got back to work. So, unless something awful happened I still should be ready to leave on time. Roy just about had his machine straightened out so he would be able to help me. He sure had trouble with his though.

It griped me a lot that I had to take a vacation down there rather than at home with Betty and Marybeth. To make the best of the situation, I thought I could get caught up with my correspondence and I hoped to go see some of the historic places of interest that upcoming week around Mexico City. I could have gone to Acapulco too but I didn't feel like it. I didn't want to spend the money and there was rumor that the upcoming week would be jammed with people and I didn't think I would enjoy it anyway without Betty. I just wanted to be home.

While I was off from work that Holy Week I did a few things. I went to the Union church in Mexico City. It was Palm Sunday and they had communion. St. Matthew's always had communion on Easter, but the Union church had it on Palm Sunday. They also took in quite a few new members and it was surprising to see how many of them were from different parts of the US and many other countries in the world.

One night, I went to my first Jai alai game. It was a fast game and quite interesting but, not being able to understand much Spanish, I didn't understand the rules of the game.

Since I had been down there I heard mentioned several times that they had a beautiful race track there, so, that afternoon I went to the horse races. It really was a beautiful place and I enjoyed looking around and seeing how things were run. I bet 40 cents on six horse races and I won one race so I got most of my money back! It was fun and it sort of reminded me of a fellow that wanted to sell us a furnace on Pear Street. The fellow arrived at our door and was reading a racing form that he had in his pocket. Can you imagine me walking around with a racing form in my pocket?

When I came back from the track I was walking through the hotel lobby when I saw a fellow whom I thought looked awfully familiar. He turned around and when he saw me he said, "Don't I know you?" I said, "Yes, but I don't remember from where." It turned out that he was a fellow from Detroit who was on the Lind with me in Korea. His name is Remono and he was down there on vacation, but he was leaving the next day for Florida.

He had driven down to Florida from Detroit and on the spur of the moment decided to fly to Mexico from Florida. He wasn't married, so he decided to take a month-long vacation. We sat and talked for quite some time about old times on the Lind and it was real nice to talk about fellows like Ducky Mohn and Pigeon. This fellow hadn't gotten off the Lind until a year after I did and he had been on the ship for a year before I first got on.

Betty had baked some cookies and mailed them to me. I received them the day before but it took a little work to get them. I got up at 9 the morning of April 4th and had breakfast. Then I took a taxi to the post office, which was on the other side of town. When I got there it was all boarded up; the post office had moved. The taxi driver took me to the new address, which was at the opposite end of town. Well, I had finally made it to the correct post office but I didn't speak much Spanish so I had quite a time finding out where to get the package. Finally I gave the card that I had received saying that there was a package at the post office to a Mexican man and he took me to the fourth floor. I turned the card in at the window where they stamped it and gave it back then I had to take it to another window and wait in line there.

I finally received an invoice that informed me that I had to pay 48 cents duty tax! I then took the card and the invoice down to the second floor and gave it to the man who had sent me to the first floor to get the invoice stamped. Then I had to go back up to the second floor and see this man again and there I had to sign a book. (I also had to sign the invoice up on the fourth floor when I paid the duty). Then another man took the card and got the package. When he gave me the package I had to sign another book.

Then we went back to the man with the first book and he wanted to see my passport. Then he wrote the number of the package and the number of the passport in the book and then after all of that, we had to go see the customs man. I was surprised that he didn't open the package! Instead he signed the invoice and I was finally free to leave with the package. I gave the Mexican man a three pesos tip that made him very happy. I would probably still be there if he hadn't helped me! I wondered how much of an ordeal I would have to go through when I wanted to leave Mexico.

Frank Romas had given me an address of a doll factory where I thought I could get some nice dolls so I went there but they were closed because of Holy Week.

The previous night, after supper, I sat in the lobby and talked to Dr. Streeter and another old gentleman from Chicago who was an advertising agent for several magazines and who had been to Lancaster and New Holland the previous November on a business trip. We sat and talked until about 11:30. I hadn't expected the Lapes to return from Acapulco until that day but the previous night about 10:30pm they came in through the lobby. They said it was too hot down there for one thing, and the first day some boy threw a rock through their windshield and that set them back about two weeks' pay. Their insurance wasn't good in Mexico. Now I was really glad that I hadn't gone.

On Wednesday, April 6 Roy and I worked all day and we were going to work the next day, and he was even talking about working Friday morning but I didn't know for sure whether we would or not. Those couple of extra days would help a lot to get finished on time.

I checked with the airline and they told me I'd better make reservations two or three weeks ahead of time. So I made my reservations that weekend for May 1. Then if I got done earlier or later I could have it changed. It sure felt good to make plans to go home. The time just didn't seem to be going fast enough!

I had killed half a day by going out to see the Guadeloupe Shrine. It was a famous Mexican Shrine and it was quite interesting to see. I saw some of the poorer class people crawl on their hands and knees from the gates all the way up to the alter which was a distance of about two city blocks. I took the poor man's trip out there. I went by bus. The bus ride took about a half hour each direction and it cost 2 cents one way. The whole trip cost me four cents.

Even Mrs. Lape was running around doing some last minute shopping. She said she worried that one day we would come home from work and tell her to start packing and she wouldn't have all of her shopping done. We worked again that day and got quite a bit accomplished.

On Saturday April 9 I celebrated that the week was finally over. It seemed to drag by slowly! We didn't work Good Friday but we did work all day Saturday. I was happy that we worked three days that week. It was Roy's suggestion, not mine. We got quite a bit accomplished too, so if everything went well I would be ready to run my machine the next Saturday. I figured I would be home by May 1. Gosh, only three more weeks! Wouldn't that be wonderful?

On Good Friday a 60 year old gentleman and I took a trolley ride out to San Angelo, a little town outside of Mexico City. This man was the one I mentioned before that I talked to in the lobby at night with Dr. Streeter. His name was Chadwick and, as I said before, he was an advertising agent from Chicago. He worked about nine months out of the year and then spent three months down there in Mexico all by himself. San Angelo was a little historic town with a market place and an old church that was built in 1600. There was a famous monument of Alvaro Obregon whom was one of their famous Presidents. We had an interesting trip and it helped to pass some time

235

away. I couldn't do any shopping though because most of the stores were closed.

On the Easter morning of April 10 I took a taxi to church but it was so crowded I couldn't get inside. So I decided to walk back towards town. On the way back to town, I passed the zoo so I thought it would be a good way to kill some time. I spent a couple of hours walking around admiring the animals and scenery. It is a pretty nice zoo and I believe it was about the same size as the Philadelphia zoo. I got back to the hotel about 2:30 in the afternoon. As I was walking back to the hotel, I noticed that all of the parks were filled with families with a lot of children. Sunday was always family day in Mexico especially on Easter Sunday!

On the evening of April 12 I went down to the Air France office but the only reservation I could get was for Friday April 29. All other dates around that had been filled. Now, all I had to do was get my machine running by that time! The plane would leave at 8am so I would have to be at the airport at 6:30am. That left about 17 more days before I would be flying home. I could hardly wait! It would be great to get back home and see Betty and Marybeth and the, soon to be, new addition to our family.

On April 15 I started knitting and everything went along fine. The next morning one of the owners went to Textile in Reading to look at the new 75 gauge machine. They were thinking of buying four of them.

I received a letter from Betty right after Easter and she had said that Dad had to work on Easter but that Mr. & Mrs. Willis invited everyone over for Easter dinner. Eleanor Miller stopped by to visit on Saturday before Easter and Eleanor, Betty and Marybeth had colored eggs that night.

On Easter Sunday, Mr. Willis picked up Betty, Marybeth, Eleanor and Mom about two in the afternoon and took them over for dinner at their house. Dorothy Willis was there for dinner and according to Betty, Marybeth took quite a shine to Dorothy. Dorothy took a position in Washington, DC as a Children's Librarian for the public library there.

On my last night I went bowling. There was another hosiery mill next door to Media Perfecta. Roy Lape worked there for five years. Every time we saw some of the knitters from that factory they asked us to go along bowling with them. We had never gone but we decided to that last night. We had a very nice time although I don't remember how well I bowled.

236

I received a letter the following day from John Fidler the inspector that I worked next to when I was in the Borematic department before I came to Mexico. He said that things had slowed down at Textile again. They were back to five days a week and he said that my inspection plate, where I had worked in the Borematic department, was still empty. Wouldn't that be something if I went back there again?

Betty wrote a letter to me on April 21 and she mentioned that the 19 of April was her brother's birthday and that she and her mother had each sent him five dollars. About 7 o'clock that evening, they got a phone call from Buddy saying that he and his wife were coming for a visit. They arrived in Chester about 10:30 that evening and stayed all night. They were to leave the next morning at 9:30 in the morning but, since they sat up and talked until three in the morning, they didn't leave until the 9:12 pm train the next evening. Betty said that Frank's wife Sylvia seemed to be very nice. She said they seemed suited for each other and they looked well together.

Sylvia had a dark complexion, large dark eyes and black hair, which she wore in an upswing. She was very attractive and wore long, dangling earrings. Frank was growing a mustache and goatee. Betty said they made quite a striking couple and would fit in well in Greenwich Village. I had always thought that Frank was a snappy dresser with lots of style and if Sylvia was the same way I was sure that they would get along fine. Frank told Betty that there was going to be an Art Show in Greenwich Village at the end of May and that he would be showing some of his pictures and work down there with the hopes of selling some of his pictures and, hopefully, making a name for himself. He claimed that some weeks he made $60 from the sale of his pictures.

It was good that I would be leaving Mexico on the 29th because I found out that May 1st would be their Labor Day and it could get pretty wild with shootings and so forth. So, I would be leaving just in time!

I had a nice surprise while I was at work the day before. Frank Romas came in to see me. He had received a telegram from the owner of the mill that he was to start Monday the 25 of April instead of May 1 so he arrived in Mexico City the day before. I hadn't expected to see him before I left but what a nice surprise! We went to a movie together on my last night.

On Sunday April 24, and probably my last Sunday in Mexico before I would leave for home, I went with the Lapes, Dr. Streeter and Mr. Chadfield up to "Max's Place" where we went for Sunday breakfast in the country. We wanted to go there for the last time to say goodbye. Mr. Chadfield had been planning to leave the same day that I was except he was going by train. Dr. Streeter would then leave on May 1 by airplane.

After breakfast, Roy took us for a nice ride in the country to a couple of neighboring towns. We had a really nice trip and the weather was hot but beautiful. I had expected to arrive in Chester that Friday night. All I had to do was pack and do a few things at work. My machine seemed to be doing fine. I just had to say goodbye to everyone.

84

Chester

After saying farewell to everyone I enjoyed a safe plane ride back to New York on Air France. I soon found myself back in Chester, PA on the Friday evening of April 29th. I was finally reunited with Betty, Marybeth and Mom and Pop. It had been a long three months but it sure was good to be back home with everyone and the way Betty looked it wouldn't be long until there was another member of the family. I couldn't believe how much Marybeth had grown and matured.

The next day Betty had a list of things that we needed to do before the baby came. On the top of her list was her appointment with Dr. Niemitz to talk about her RH factor. Betty had type A blood with an RH negative and I had type A blood with an RH positive. When Marybeth was born we were told that this is the worst combination of blood you can have and that sometimes you have what they call a blue baby and if that happened they would have to give the baby a blood transfusion. When Marybeth was born Mom said she was really dark but they didn't give her a transfusion and everything turned out alright.

Betty said that they were making arrangements for this baby to have an ambulance and crew standing by at the county so that if there was a problem after the birth they could rush the baby to St. Christopher Hospital in Philadelphia for a transfusion.

When Betty felt the baby coming, we decided to go to the hospital in the afternoon. We spent the rest of the day there but not much happened. In the evening, the doctor told me that I might as well go home because nothing was going to happen that night. I eventually went home and went to bed. About 11:30 pm the phone rang and it was the doctor. He said "Congratulations, you have a little boy." I thanked him and asked him if they were both alright and he said "yes." I went back to sleep and, believe you me, Betty never let me forget that!

That next morning I went into the hospital and as soon as they let me in her room I went to see Betty. I actually went to see where the babies were so I could see our new son because I had to wait to get in to see Betty. I found him and I was sure that he was the most beautiful baby there. Thank heaven there wasn't any problem with the RH factor so nothing special had to be done. Both Betty and Steve were doing fine. When I arrived home from Mexico I had some time accumulated, so I could take off from work with pay and I didn't have to report for work in Reading right away. I took some time to just stay home and get used to being with Betty, Marybeth and Kenneth Steven Fidler, our new son.

I don't remember just when we moved back to our house in Reading and when I started work again but I do know that Steven was christened in June at St. Matthew's Lutheran Church in Reading, PA. Betty's parents, Francis and Elizabeth McBride, were his sponsors.

Epilogue

I am now 88 years old. My wife Betty passed away in 2009 after a long and happy marriage. My children are grown and doing well. Life has been good.

My ninety-six years old Uncle Will, when asked long ago what he attributed his long life to said, "Just keep moving." I play golf once or twice a week and with my son and daughter-in-law when they visit; go to the health club; take care of my daughter's standard poodle, Jack, when she travels; and spend time on my computer and projects like this. I follow Uncle Will's advice and "just keep moving…"

Lancaster, PA
November 2013

KENNETH H. FIDLER

Rate/Rank
SOM3

Service Branch
USN 04/1943 - 12/1945
USN 09/1950 - 12/1951

Born
3/2/1925
READING, PA

- USS LOY DE-160 / APD-56
- NAVAL TRAINING STATION, SAMPSON, NY
- SONAR SCHOOL, KEY WEST, FL
- USS WALLACE L. LIND DD-703

- NAVY UNIT COMMENDATION
- AMERICAN CAMPAIGN MEDAL
- EUROPEAN-AFRICAN-MIDDLE EASTERN CAMPAIGN MEDAL
- WORLD WAR II VICTORY MEDAL

USS Wallace L Lind DD 703

USS Loy APD 56

USS Loy DE 160

Made in the USA
Charleston, SC
05 January 2014